Christ all-sufficient

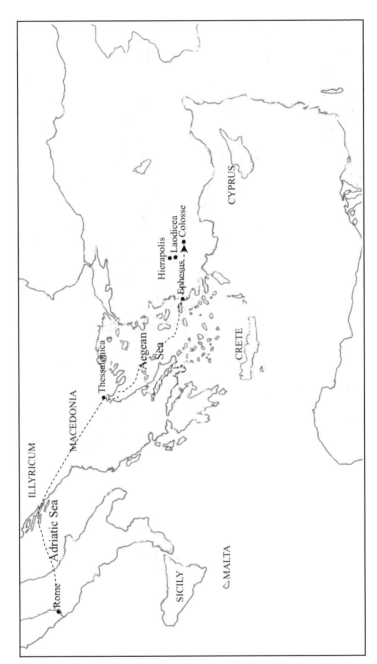

Map showing the location of Colosse and the probable route taken by Tychicus to deliver the letters

Christ all-sufficient

Colossians and Philemon simply explained

J. Philip Arthur

EVANGELICAL PRESS

EVANGELICAL PRESS
Faverdale North, Darlington, DL3 0PH, England

e-mail: sales@evangelicalpress.org

Evangelical Press USA
P. O. Box 825, Webster, New York 14580, USA

e-mail: usa.sales@evangelicalpress.org

web: http://www.evangelicalpress.org

First published 2007

British Library Cataloguing in Publication Data available

ISBN-13 978 0 85234 655 6   ISBN 0 85234 655 7

Printed and bound in Great Britain by Biddles Ltd, King's Lynn,
Norfolk

This book is dedicated
to the one whose 'worth is far above rubies'
and to whom I owe a debt that could never be repaid.

Contents

Part 2: Philemon

Preface

When I first became aware of Paul's epistle to the Colossians, relatively early in my Christian life, I fell in love with it because of the exalted description of the Lord Jesus Christ that occupies much of chapter 1. Once called to the full-time Christian ministry, I knew that sooner or later I would be drawn to preach a series of sermons on this compelling book. As always, I am very much in debt to the members of Free Grace Baptist Church in Lancaster for the patient hearing they gave to these messages when they eventually appeared in 2003 and 2004. Their patience was all the greater this time round because an emergency meant that the series was interrupted for six months. In due course what was a modest series of sermons has become a modest book and I am very grateful to the people who encourage me every Sunday of the year with their loyal attendance upon my ministry and constant prayers.

In similar vein, I would like to thank David Clark of Evangelical Press for his encouragement and the members of the EP board who reviewed the manuscript for their hard work and for shrewd and helpful suggestions while this book was in its early stages. I have tried hard to take all of the advice that was proffered and am sure that the book is much the better for that. The very few instances where I have differed from their judgement do not make me any the less grateful for a great deal of thoughtful and gracious help.

While this book was in its gestation period, I picked the brains of several authors who have written better books than this one. Their names, and the titles of the books in question, are in the appendix. Scripture quotations throughout are from the New King James Version of the Holy Scriptures, unless otherwise stated. It is possible that I have unwittingly quoted from various sources without giving proper recognition. If any such quotations are brought to my attention, I gladly undertake to correct the matter if the book is ever reprinted.

My wife, Barbara, has borne patiently with a husband whose relationship with a keyboard has sometimes resembled that of a galley-slave with an oar. I am grateful to her for many things, not least among which is her capacity to blunt the edge of my frustration. Likewise, my three sons, James, Luke and Sam, all have the happy knack of keeping my feet on the ground and regularly provide refreshing doses of normality. The blame for the many imperfections of this book rests with me, and with me alone! But if, in the course of time, it helps even one reader to understand the mind of Paul a little better and to grasp why the fulness that we have in Christ is more than sufficient for the church in any age, the effort involved in writing it will have been amply rewarded.

J. Philip Arthur,
August 2007

Part I:
Colossians

Introduction to Colossians

What kind of place was Colosse?

The letter that we know as the epistle to the Colossians is short, a mere four chapters. Nevertheless, it is packed with good things. Not a word is wasted. It was written by the apostle Paul to a group of Christians in a town named Colosse (also spelt Colossae). This town was situated in a region known in ancient times as Phrygia. When the Romans conquered it they incorporated it into their province of Asia. (This region is now known as Anatolia in modern Turkey.) For several centuries, Colosse was a thriving town in the valley of the River Lycus, on an important east-west trading route. To the west, on the coast, lay the important seaport of Ephesus. Ten miles downstream, in the direction of Ephesus, lay two neighbouring towns which faced each other across the Lycus — Laodicea and Hierapolis. By the time that Paul wrote this letter, Colosse had seen better days. It was in a state of slow decline, while Laodicea and Hierapolis had begun to flourish. When the region was conquered by the Turks, the inhabitants deserted Colosse. There is nothing there now but ruins. At the time when this epistle was written a large Jewish community had existed there for some time. It made a significant contribution to both the economic and spiritual life of the town.

It is unlikely that Paul had ever been there, but the Christian gospel began to make inroads in Colosse while he was in nearby Ephesus. Paul spent two action-packed years in that bustling city, using a lecture hall owned by a man named Tyrannus during the lunchtime siesta. During that time a man named Epaphras, a native of Colosse, was converted, probably under Paul's ministry. This man matured quickly and soon became a spiritual leader of real calibre. He became the evangelist of the Lycus Valley, and churches sprang up in all three towns.

Why did Paul write Colossians?

Although Paul had not founded the church in Colosse, he wrote this letter in response to the fact that Epaphras had travelled all the way to Rome while Paul was under house arrest. The arrival of his friend alerted the apostle to the church and naturally he wanted to know how things stood. It seemed that there were substantial grounds for encouragement. On the whole, things were going well. There was, nevertheless, a problem, and it was this that prompted Paul to write.

There is a clue to the problem in 2:6-7, where Paul challenged the believers: 'As you therefore have received Christ Jesus the Lord, so walk in him, rooted and built up in him and established in the faith, as you have been taught, abounding in it with thanksgiving.' It seemed that there was a real danger that an impressionable young church might be seduced away from uncomplicated and straightforward devotion to Christ. Their great need was to stay loyal to the gospel they had already heard and embraced. This explains the apostle's warning in 2:8: 'Beware lest anyone cheat you through philosophy and empty deceit, according to the tradition of men, according to the basic principles of the

world, and not according to Christ.' It seems that Epaphras
had detected a new mood in the church, a worrying tendency
to be influenced by currents of thought from outside, from
society at large as it then was. The details may vary, but
today's churches face exactly the same problem. The church
is often influenced by the world more than it knows.

What had brought matters to a head was that some of the
teachers in the church had adopted a number of new emphases. Among other things, they had begun to stress the need
for 'fulness', arguing in effect that the believers in Colosse
were lacking something. They implied that Epaphras'
message had been all right as far as it went, but the believers
would not be complete until they received the vital extra that
was missing. (In Colosse, this appears to have been some
form of mystical knowledge or enlightenment. This was a
common view in the Greek world of the eastern Mediterranean. Two centuries later it had grown into a much more
highly developed form of spirituality known to us as Gnosticism.) At heart, the new teachers were elitist. According to
them, the gospel preached by Epaphras was all well and
good, but only up to a point. First-century Colossians needed
the full gospel. They needed Christ, but they also needed to
be 'in the know'. The same syndrome is at work in the
evangelical scene today. If all you have done is to trust
Christ for salvation, you can be left with the impression that
you are, in effect, an inferior Christian and that you will not
be complete until you have undergone a particular experience, acquired a certain gift, and so on.

There is also evidence within the letter that the new
teachers were emphasizing the necessity of keeping rules.
These included Jewish rituals such as circumcision
(2:11-12), Jewish dietary laws (2:16) and Sabbath regulations. It is not surprising that this mentality was taking
hold. There is always something in human nature that wants
to reduce religion to a set of rules, when it ought to be a

relationship with God. A religion made up of rules ceases to be a matter of the heart; it is all about doing things. The man who keeps most of the rules can be proud of his achievement. What God thinks about that kind of mindset is another matter.

Finally, it is also worth noting that the new teachers had a lot to say about supernatural powers. For them, true spirituality involved gaining the mastery over the forces of evil and gaining the help of the angels in order to do so. I have met modern Christians who see spiritual warfare not so much as a battle against temptation and sin, but about our getting involved in duels between angels and demons.

The most important consequence of all this, however, was that it would wean people away from Christ in subtle ways by making them preoccupied with other things in addition to him. This is what gives Colossians its particular fascination. In order to counter this new emphasis, Paul wrote a letter that is full of Christ. Read it, and it will work wonders for your confidence. In a variety of ways it makes the point that Christ is magnificent, that nothing can compare with him and if we have Jesus, we have enough.

Why study Colossians?

This letter has much to say to modern Christians. It will repay everyone who makes the effort to get to know it.

1. It is for Christians who want to stand firm

One essential if we are not to be shaky Christians, but the kind who are well rooted in the faith, is clarity of mind about the essentials of Christianity. We need a clear grasp of what the gospel really is, and therefore what a real Christian is. Colossians reminds us that Christianity is, at heart, a relationship with Jesus Christ, the most fascinating and fulfilling person in the universe. Like believers in first-century Colosse, Christians today face the subtle temptation to conclude that Christ by himself is not enough. Paul made much of Christ in this epistle in order to face down this threat. This is an epistle with an extremely high view of Jesus Christ. It leaves us in no doubt that the Christian life is a matter of being united to him, of knowing him and being known by him, of loving him and being loved by him.

2. It is for jaded Christians who need a spiritual tonic

Colossians is so full of Christ that it lifts the spirits. Sooner or later all believers go through dry patches when everything seems flat and stale and their spiritual vitality has become listless and torpid. Nothing does us more good at such times than to be reminded of just what a treasure we have in our Saviour — to see, as Samuel Rutherford said, that 'He is his lone self a sufficient heaven.'

3. It is for those who care about spiritual excellence

I have never come across a Christian who did not want to be a better Christian, to respond to the love of Christ with a more consistent level of devotion than he or she had shown in the past. This longing may be fleeting, but all true follow-ers of Jesus know at least something of it. We are also conscious that God expects no less from us. His will for our lives is our sanctification (1 Thess. 4:3). Our attempts to grow in grace, however, sometimes fall foul of the fact that there are different theories in circulation as to what consti-tutes Christian growth. Which of the several different schools of sanctification on offer is actually in the right? Colossians was written partly to highlight one false view that was current in the first century and to point believers to what is really involved if we are to be new people in Christ. It is full of help and encouragement for those who want their lives to count for God.

4. It is for Christians who care about their churches

Do our churches have a future? Assuming that Jesus does not return first, will they survive into the twenty-second century with their evangelical character intact? Regrettably, some modern Christians have experienced the very thing that Epaphras feared might befall the church in Colosse. They have seen their churches gradually infiltrated and captured by unscrupulous people, so that the character of each church and its message for the community are no longer what they were at the outset. Colossians not only shows us something of the character and the methods of such people; it also reminds us that the best remedy for error is a heartfelt love for Christ and the robust proclamation of his truth.

5. It is for Christians who care about relationships

Bringing the whole of life under the lordship of Christ involves giving thought and care to ensuring that our dealings with the other people in our lives bring glory to God. This is particularly important in the West, where the cult of the individual often functions as a cloak for rampant self-promotion and self-assertion. Colossians has much to say about the corporate dimension of the Christian life, about the kind of graces that make for harmony within the local fellowship, and even the kind of character we should display to those on the outside of the Christian community. There is also helpful emphasis on relationships within the family and the workplace.

1.
Paul greets the Colossians

Please read Colossians 1:1-8

Greetings (1:1-2)

Paul followed the usual custom of the day and used the formula: 'The writer to the reader, greetings.' This can seem odd to modern Westerners who are used to finding the writer's name at the very end of a letter, but letters in the ancient world were written on scrolls rolled up from the bottom. The sender needed to place his name at the top!

1. The writer and his fellow worker

It is worth noting that Paul made each part of the customary formula of his day distinctively Christian. He began with his name. His title, **'an apostle of Jesus Christ'**, was a reminder to his readers that he wrote with authority. He was more than a concerned friend. His experience on the Damascus road meant that he was as much an eyewitness of Christ's resurrection as the original disciples. He was a special ambassador from the risen Lord, carrying the King's commission. Moreover, apostleship was not something that he had aspired to, or attained through the sustained pursuit of spiritual excellence. It was bestowed upon him **'by the will of God'**.

Timothy was with Paul at the time of writing and was therefore included in the greeting. A native of Lystra with a Gentile father and a Jewish mother, Timothy had been converted on Paul's second missionary journey. In spite of his physical weakness and occasional emotional frailty, he had become indispensable to Paul. The apostle confided to the church at Philippi: 'I have no one like-minded, who will sincerely care for your state. For all seek their own, not the things which are of Christ Jesus. But you know his proven character, that as a son with his father he served with me in the gospel' (Phil. 2:20-22).

2. The readers to whom the letter was addressed

Paul went on to describe his readers as **'the saints and faithful brethren in Christ ... in Colosse'**. Our word **'saints'** translates a Greek term meaning 'holy ones', people whom God has called out from the world and set apart for his own use. It does not mean 'eminent Christians'; it simply means 'Christians'. **'Brethren'** translates the Greek word *'adelphoi'*, which can mean either 'brothers' or 'brothers and sisters', depending on the context. As it is addressed here to the members of a church, it refers to them all, males and females of all ages. **'Faithful'** is the same word that is used in verse 7 to describe the calibre of Epaphras' service for God. By calling his readers **'faithful brethren'**, Paul indicated that he thought that his readers were Christians of proven character.

3. The form of greeting

He went on to express his desire that they might enjoy grace and peace **'from God our Father and the Lord Jesus Christ'**. In writing as he did, Paul echoed the conventional form of words in use at the time. Instead of the Greek word for 'greeting' *(chairein)*, the apostle used a similar-sounding word, which means 'grace' *(charis)*. To this he added the Greek version of the familiar Jewish greeting, '*Shalom*', or 'peace'. This was much more than mere formal politeness. 'Grace' and 'peace' are two of the loveliest words in the Christian vocabulary.

'Grace' is the undeserved favour of God, his kindness to those who merit his wrath and condemnation. Human sinfulness means that we are entitled to feel the weight of divine anger against sin, but God in his grace has sent his Son into the world to live and die in the place of sinners. Peace follows on naturally from grace. Because God is gracious, it is gloriously possible for those who have offended him to be reconciled to him. Paul's readers in Colosse had already experienced the grace of God in their lives. Had this not been the case, they would not have been Christians at all. But if God saves us by his grace, he also keeps us by his grace. The help that Christians receive to live for God each day is gracious help. That is why Christians in the first century were in the habit of commending one another to the grace of God (see Acts 15:40). In effect, Paul expressed a heartfelt longing that the God who had been gracious to the believers in Colosse at the outset of their Christian lives would continue to sustain and help them in the future.

The same logic is at work in what is effectively a prayer that God would grant them **'peace'**. In one sense, peace was something they had already experienced. Because of all that Jesus Christ had achieved in living and dying for his people, where once there was enmity and estrangement, now there was peace. Paul's readers knew that, since God no longer has a quarrel against his people, they could be at peace within and among themselves. It follows that this word 'peace' involves more than the absence of hostilities between God and man. Paul was giving expression to a deeply held wish that his friends might increasingly enjoy what Leon Morris calls 'a flourishing state of soul'.

Thanksgiving (1:3-8)

It was typical of Paul to give thanks for his fellow-believers. We often find this note near the start of his letters. The direction of his thanksgiving is important. It is not that he thanked the Colossians themselves for having attained certain spiritual qualities, but rather that he was grateful to **'the God and Father of our Lord Jesus Christ'** (1:3) for all that he had done in the lives of these Christians to produce such qualities.

1. The Colossians were true Christians

Moreover, his thanks were more than an expression of heartfelt gratitude. He made them known in order to address a pastoral need. Paul knew, from what Epaphras had told him, that the Colossian believers had had their confidence in the simplicity of the gospel subtly undermined by the new teachers. It is likely that they had begun to feel insecure. It is the same nowadays. When you repeatedly hear a line of teaching that leaves you to make the inference that you are lacking the vital element needed to make you a 'full' Christian, you begin to wonder whether you are a real Christian at all. This is the concern that Paul addressed in verses 3-5.

His statement that he was **'praying always'** (1:3) makes it clear that Paul prayed frequently and regularly for his friends in Colosse. This in itself is a challenge to modern Christians. It is easy enough to finish a conversation with a cheery, 'I'll be praying for you.' It is quite another thing to see it through. The thrust of these verses is that on those occasions when Paul did pray for the Christians in Colosse, he thanked God for them because he was confident that they really were true believers. This reassurance must have meant a great deal to them.

This inevitably leaves the reader asking an important question, one that we do well to ask ourselves. What qualities make a real Christian, and are they present in my own life? Paul mentions a group of three such qualities — faith, love and hope. We often find Paul referring to one or more of these graces and sometimes to all three. For example, he did so on other occasions when he gave thanks to God for all that he was doing in the lives of a group of Christians. To believers in Thessalonica he wrote, 'We give thanks to God always for you all, making mention of you in our prayers, remembering without ceasing your work of faith, labour of love, and patience of hope in our Lord Jesus Christ in the sight of our God and Father' (1 Thess. 1:2-3). Paul was not alone in linking these three words. Other examples can be found elsewhere in the New Testament,[1] perhaps because these three qualities provide a summary of what it is to be a Christian. Whether in first-century Colosse or anywhere else, it is wonderful to belong to a gospel church because the world at large is faithless, loveless and hopeless.

By **'faith'** (1:4) Paul meant a solid conviction that certain things are true, combined with a willingness to venture everything on those truths. It involves believing that the Bible is absolutely right, not only about the human predicament, our deep sinfulness and guilt before God, but about the only solution to it, the cross of Christ. It also involves entrusting ourselves to Christ crucified, handing over our lives, our whole selves and our eternal destinies to him.

We should also note that Paul did not mean faith in the abstract, faith as a power or principle. The believers in Colosse put their faith **'in Christ'** (1:4). Everyday experience will tell you that your capacity for trust will let you down if you place it in someone who is untrustworthy.

Entrust yourself to Jesus, and you won't regret it. Entrust yourself body and soul to anything or anyone else instead of him, and tragedy will ensue.

Paul had also learned of a second quality that could be detected in his friends in Colosse. Besides their faith, he also thanked God for their **'love for all the saints'** (1:4). This kind of love is one way of proving that the faith we claim to have is genuine. Faith alone saves, but the faith that saves is never alone: 'We know that we have passed from death to life, because we love the brethren. He who does not love his brother abides in death' (1 John 3:14). What made the church in Colosse impressive was the fact that this love was not selective. They did not confine themselves to loving the saints who were easy to get on with, or the ones with money or influence. Of course, it is not realistic to be equally drawn to all our fellow Christians. Each of us will 'gel' more readily with some than others. But we can resolve to do everything in our power for the good of all. Often, once we have decided to love someone and begun to live that decision out in practical ways, the feelings will follow.

Thirdly, Paul went on to mention the **'hope'** that is **'laid up'** for believers **'in heaven'** (1:5). The way that Paul described this hope almost suggests that his readers needed some assurance on this matter, perhaps because the new-comers had been teaching things that called into question the Christian's confidence in a blessed future. Firstly, a hope that is located in heaven is beyond the reach of anything that might threaten it. No combination of spiritual foes can undermine this hope, for it has, in effect, been stored in the safest location of all. Secondly, Paul's comment that this hope was something they had already **'heard before'** (1:5) was essentially an endorsement of Epaphras over against those who had intruded themselves into the church with a very different message from his. The founder of the church had instructed them correctly about the Christian's hope, whereas those who threw it into doubt had not.

2. The Colossians had heard the true gospel

Paul also wanted to assure his readers that not only were they true Christians, but also that they had heard the true gospel. Epaphras had not fobbed them off with a partial or inadequate version of it. It is unlikely that many of the believers in Colosse would have heard Paul himself. Some, influenced by the new teachers, would therefore be tempted to jump to conclusions that Epaphras was not teaching all that Paul taught. Paul went on to address this concern in verses 5-8.

Verse 5 closes with a complex phrase, **'the word of the truth of the gospel'**. Every element in it is important. **'Word'** makes a simple but important point. In the first century, the gospel was presented verbally. Epaphras had won a hearing with his fellow Colossians by talking to them. Nowadays in some circles the gospel is acted, danced or mimed. Circus clowns and body-builders are also pressed into service. Are such approaches popular because they are not as confrontational as preaching, or indeed straight talk in informal settings? Paul coupled the word **'truth'** with **'gospel'** to make the point that the Christians in Colosse had not heard an incomplete presentation of the Christian message that would need rounding off. The same point is emphasized in verse 6. They had **'heard and knew the grace of God in truth'**. The Colossians had no need to fear that what they had learned from Epaphras had been inadequate, partial, or even false.

Another reason why they could feel confident in Epaphras' message was that the message that came to them had also been heard **'in all the world'** (1:6). At this point we need to appreciate that Paul was not indulging himself in wild exaggeration. At the time of writing, few people would have had a more complete grasp of the true spread of the gospel than he did. We know from his writing elsewhere that he was painfully aware that much of the world was still virgin territory as far as the gospel was concerned. There were regions where no one yet knew the name of Christ and, if possible, Paul wanted to reach them first (Rom. 15:20). Nevertheless, there was already a growing body of towns and cities with an established Christian presence, enough to make comparisons appropriate. Believers in Colosse could be assured that, far from having heard an incomplete version of the gospel that would need to be fleshed out with important details that Epaphras had missed, they had heard the same gospel that all other Christians everywhere had heard. It was not as though others had heard the whole truth but they had heard somewhat less than the full gospel.

In passing we should note here that, though Paul's primary purpose was to reassure the Colossian believers, there is a strong hint of a note that we find elsewhere in the New Testament. The gospel is not something which has only a limited, local appeal, as though people of one cultural background were disposed to give it a hearing while others from a different background would be indifferent to it. The gospel is a dynamic force well able to transform people of all nations, languages and cultures.

In the same way, the Colossians could reflect with encouragement on the thought that the gospel that was **'bringing forth fruit'** (1:6) in their town was equally productive elsewhere. We first meet the idea that the gospel grows in the hearts of men and women in the same way that seed grows in the ground in certain of Jesus' parables, notably the parable of the sower and the soils (Luke 8:4-8,11-15). Paul may have had two kinds of growth in mind. Perhaps, on the one hand, he was thinking of the way that the gospel can produce a harvest of good deeds in the life of those who hear it, what he called elsewhere 'fruits of righteousness' (Phil. 1:11). On the other hand, he may equally have been thinking of fruit as a graphic way to describe a harvest of souls — in other words, the fact that people were coming to faith in Christ in numbers. Whatever kind of spiritual fruit Paul had in view, the same conclusion holds good. If Epaphras' evangelism had the same results as those of other evangelists in other places, whether in terms of evangelistic success or of transformed lives, he must have preached the same gospel as they did.

This endorsement for Epaphras and his ministry is stated clearly in verse 7. The Colossians had **'learned'** the gospel from him. Paul's choice of verb is unusual here. Ordinarily we find Paul writing of Christians 'believing', 'hearing' or 'obeying' the gospel. It is likely that his choice of words was deliberate and that he intended to suggest that Epaphras had done his work well, providing thorough and systematic teaching of Christian truth. Indeed, far from being an ineffective communicator who had left the job unfinished, he was **'a faithful minister of Christ'**. (We should note in passing that the word **'minister'** is one rendering of a Greek word that would be better translated 'servant', given that in today's world, the word 'minister' often has overtones of the 'clergy', the employees of various religious denominations.) Paul used the same word on other occasions to describe Timothy (1 Thess. 3:2) and Tychicus (4:7).

The same idea is even present in verse 8. Epaphras had told Paul and Timothy about the Colossians' **'love in the Spirit'** — that is to say, it was a love that was supernatural in origin, a love that no one could produce by himself, but the Holy Spirit had been at work in Colosse in such a way that the believers there showed clear evidence of it. Surely a man who told Paul the truth about the Colossians was a man of integrity who could be relied upon to teach them the truth about the great message of sin and salvation?

It may seem tempting to think that quantities of ink used to buttress the reputation of a first-century evangelist have little to say to modern people. This is light years from the truth. Modern people still need to know what the true gospel is and they still need people of calibre to explain it to them. There is a vacancy in every town for an Epaphras.

Conclusion

Before we leave this opening section of Paul's letter to the Christian believers who made up the church in first-century Colosse, it is worth noting that we are given a glimpse of one theme that preoccupied Paul more than any other, the gospel. (The fact that he said, in Romans 1:16, that he was 'not ashamed of the gospel of Christ' means that he was actually proud of it, that it thrilled him to the core.)

We see it, first of all, in the effect that it has on human lives, producing people characterized by faith in Christ, love for one another and a vibrant hope for the future. We do well to ask ourselves whether the gospel that we have encountered has had that kind of effect on us. Secondly, we also see it in Paul's defence of his colleague Epaphras, where he has given us a portrait of the kind of person who can proclaim this life-changing gospel with credibility. There is no doubt that Paul was a man of one thing. Today's churches would be well served if modern believers had even a little of his clarity and intensity of focus.

2.
Paul prays for the Colossians

Please read Colossians 1:9-14

In the original Greek, Paul begins a sentence in verse 9 that does not end until verse 20. This enormous sentence has 218 words. It is a substantial block of writing. This meaty chunk of prose is made up of two distinct sections, each with its own main theme. In our next chapter, we shall examine the second of these two sections, which runs from verse 15 onwards. In that passage the apostle deals with the greatness of Christ, the splendour of his being, his majestic role in the creation of the universe and the redemption of his people. We shall learn from those verses that Christ is sufficient. He is the only Saviour that his people could ever need. Moreover, it is the purpose of Almighty God that his glorious Son should have the pre-eminence in all things (1:18).

The introduction to Paul's prayer (1:9)

We begin, however, by examining the section that runs from verse 9 to verse 14, where Paul continues a theme he had already begun in verse 3.

1. Why Paul prayed for them

As he wrote these words, Paul was under house arrest in
Rome. He had received a visit from Epaphras, the evangelist
who had planted the church in Colosse. On the whole,
Epaphras had given an encouraging report. God was at work
in Colosse. That is why Paul struck such a positive note in
verses 3-4, giving thanks to God for the reality of their 'faith
in Christ Jesus' and their 'love for all the saints'.

At the same time, Epaphras was concerned that his work
was being subtly undermined. The Christian church was
barely one generation old, yet new teachers had emerged
with a seductive new approach that was in danger of attract-
ing a sizeable following. This new teaching was essentially
an attempt to modify the Christian message, to make it more
palatable to first-century people by blending it with various
ideas that were widely accepted at the time. This problem
has never gone away. We face it today. In every age the
church has come under pressure to allow her message to be
shaped by the intellectual fashions of the day.

This, then, was the situation that prompted Paul to write
this letter to a church that he had never visited in person. His
first concern was to let them know that he thanked God for
them. This in itself would be very reassuring. The new
teachers had left the believers in Colosse with the nagging
fear that they might not be proper Christians at all. Paul,
however, was satisfied with their credentials and confident
that Epaphras had been a responsible evangelist.

2. How Paul prayed for them

Now, from verse 9 onwards, building on his words of heartfelt thanksgiving, Paul wanted his readers to understand that
he prayed for them. His opening phrase, **'for this reason'**
(1:9), means that, in view of all that Epaphras had said about

them, in view of the sterling qualities that proved the genuineness of their faith, the very things that made Paul give heartfelt thanks to God; he did 'not cease to pray' for them (1:9). Not only did Paul pray for the Christians in Colosse, he never stopped! The phrase, **'we ... do not cease to pray for you'**, does not mean that he prayed round the clock, but rather that during his set times of prayer, the church at Colosse came up again and again. The spiritual good of these believers mattered to him. Modern Christians too need to reckon with the fact that the content of our prayers is an infallible guide to our spiritual priorities. Those things which are rarely far from our thoughts will feature most frequently in our prayers.

A prayer for fulness (1:9-10)

There is much to be gained from studying Paul's prayers. One outstanding feature of them is that spiritual concerns are always to the fore. This is not always true of our prayers for other people. We become easily absorbed with lesser things — physical health, career prospects, and so on.

In the first place, Paul wanted his readers to be **'filled with the knowledge of [God's] will in all wisdom and spiritual understanding'** (1:9). His choice of words at this point is highly significant. 'Fulness' and 'knowledge' were two of the pet themes of the new teachers who had infiltrated the church at Colosse. These men had not opposed Epaphras outright. Instead, they seem to have hinted that, while he had certainly introduced the people of Colosse to Christian basics, something more was needed. Now the time had come to move on, to take the next step, to receive the full gospel. Powerful hints were continually being dropped that they needed an experience of 'fulness'. Any believer in Colosse who wanted to belong to the spiritual elite needed 'knowledge'. This translates the Greek word *'gnosis'*. It can also be rendered 'insight'. It does not mean knowledge of the Scriptures, but a form of mystical enlightenment. Those who had it were 'in the know'. Those who didn't would be written off as spiritually second-rate. In order to acquire this 'knowledge' it was usually necessary to go through some form of initiation. A century later, a more developed form of this teaching, known as Gnosticism, became a serious problem to the churches. Even today there are believers whose confidence has been undermined because others have told them that mere repentance towards God and faith in Jesus Christ are not enough, that the message of the new birth is not the full gospel. Believers can be left with the strong impression that their lives will never really count for God until they have been through a particular experience, acquired a certain supernatural gift, and so on.

1. The knowledge of God's will

Although Paul used the vocabulary of his opponents, he had not bought into their agenda. He had a different kind of 'fulness' and 'knowledge' in mind — not something esoteric and mystical, but something hard-headed and practical. What comes to mind when you hear a phrase like 'knowing God's will'? Modern Christians tend to assume that it means discovering whom God intended them to marry, or working out which career he had in mind for them. Paul was not thinking in these terms at all. In verse 10 he explains that knowing God's will has ethical and moral consequences.

First of all, it involves walking **'worthy of the Lord'**. **'Walk'** is a common New Testament way of describing the whole direction of a person's way of life, and that life must be **'worthy'** of God. Speaking positively, this means that a Christian's lifestyle should be fitting, or appropriate. Speaking negatively, it means that nothing in a believer's life should jar, or be unseemly. We must reflect nothing but credit on Jesus.

Paul's second phrase, **'fully pleasing him'**, builds on this idea. How can we please God in every respect unless we make a systematic and thoroughgoing attempt to find out how he wants us to live? In the same way, how can we avoid what displeases him unless we take the trouble to find out what it is?

Thirdly, Paul prayed that the believers in Colosse would be **'fruitful in every good work'**. This involves a commitment to spiritual excellence right across the board. **'Every'** good work means being as comprehensive and wide-ranging as possible in our pursuit of holiness. The word **'fruitful'** has echoes of Paul's words elsewhere about the 'fruit' of the Spirit: 'love, joy, peace, long-suffering, kindness, goodness, faithfulness, gentleness, self-control' (Gal. 5:22-23). Our good works are to have a certain character. They are to be shot through with spiritual and moral worth.

Does all this seem mundane and unexciting measured against the different kinds of 'full gospel' package? It is certainly in keeping with other statements by Paul about the will of God: 'For this is the will of God, your sanctification' (1 Thess. 4:3). In Romans 12:2 the apostle writes, 'Do not be conformed to this world, but be transformed by the renewing of your mind, that you may prove what is that good and acceptable and perfect will of God.' It is God's will that we should not let the world shape the way that we think. Instead, we must commit ourselves to a businesslike policy of mind renewal, learning how to think in a Christian way, so that our behaviour will fall into line.

2. Growth in the grace that they already had

To sum up, Paul took on the new teachers head-on. Like some teachers in evangelical circles today, their pitch was essentially, 'You will never be a complete Christian until you have added this extra dimension, this new experience or gift.' In response, Paul was not advocating stagnation. Every Christian needs more. But the fulness that Christians need is not something new or different, but more of what they already have. This is what Paul had in mind when he prayed that the Colossian believers would increase **'in the knowledge of God'** (1:10). They already knew God. All Christians do. If you don't know God, you are not a Christian. But there is more of God to be known than we have yet discovered, a greater depth of love, a more intense holiness than we have yet reached. Suppose that we want to know God better. What is involved? Whenever we discover some new aspect of God's will we must modify our behaviour in line with it. If we do, God will respond to our earnestness and reveal yet more of himself to us.

We should also note that Paul prayed that every believer in Colosse would experience this growth in grace. He wanted them all to walk worthy of the Lord, to please him in all respects, and so on, whereas the new teachers in Colosse had a divisive effect on the church. In effect they were creating two classes of Christians, those with this added blessing and those without.

A prayer for power (1:11)

Paul went on to pray that his readers might be **'strengthened with all might, according to his glorious power'**. The phrase **'all might'** shows that Paul was thinking on the grand scale. It was not that he asked for the power of God to be made known to a certain limited extent, but rather that he longed to see God's power in all its fulness at work in the lives of his readers. He describes it as **'glorious power'** because, when this power is at work, it reveals the glory of the Almighty.

1. The power to persevere

It is worth noting that 'power' was another term often employed by the new teachers. Some modern evangelicals are also obsessed with it — power to heal the sick, speak in other tongues, give 'words of knowledge', drive out demons, and so on. Here at least, Paul is concerned with a different kind of power, the power to show **'patience'** in adversity and to combine **'long-suffering'** and **'joy**'. In other words, Paul asked God to give his friends moral power, the ability to live well and to go on doing so. Perhaps he understood the mind of God better than we sometimes do. God is more concerned with graces than with gifts, with our character than with our abilities. This is essentially Paul's argument in 1 Corinthians 13. Showy gifts are worthless where there is no love. A person with no unusual supernatural powers who has learned to love as God loves is Christlike; a man with all manner of dramatic abilities whose life is void of love is not. Gifts, however wonderful, are morally neutral, and God wants us to be holy.

Paul emphasizes two qualities here that he wanted every believer in Colosse, not just a favoured elite, to develop. These were **'patience'** on the one hand and **'long-suffering'** on the other. These qualities, of course, are not spectacular. A man with a reputation for the gift of prophecy will attract attention. A man who can endure bitter disappointments while keeping his faith intact may well not. Indeed, 'patience and long-suffering' only become apparent with the passage of time.

By **'patience'** Paul meant the ability to last the course, steady perseverance. It is a quality that all Christians are to cultivate. We are to 'run with endurance the race that is set before us' (Heb. 12:1). To do so is to be Christlike, since Jesus 'endured the cross' for 'the joy that was set before him' (Heb. 12:2). The believers in Colosse could also be confident that Paul was not encouraging them to manifest an aspect of Christian character that he knew nothing about himself. The apostle could certainly lay claim to patient endurance. Over the years Paul had kept going in the face of numerous trials that would have sapped the vitality of a lesser man (2 Cor. 11:22-29).

'Long-suffering' is a related quality, the ability to ride out difficult situations and bear with difficult people. It includes the ability to keep going without bitterness in the face of disappointments. It involves cultivating 'the patience of unanswered prayer'. There is nothing flashy about the power to keep going, but it is Christianity of the old school. It breeds stalwart martyrs and missionary pioneers who, like William Carey, could 'plod'. And which kind of 'power' would you prefer — the ability to produce a spectacular miracle in front of a crowd of thousands, or the ability to live out a whole lifetime without letting Jesus down?

2. Joy whatever their circumstances

We should also note that Paul was not describing the endurance of the stoic. Stoicism was a popular philosophy in the Roman world. Many people, including at least one emperor,[1] aspired to a life of emotional detachment. Paul, however, was not thinking of the kind of endurance that goes with being a man of steel, unmoved by things that would have a profound effect on the emotional lives of others. He coupled 'patience and long-suffering' with **'joy'**. He prayed that his brothers and sisters in Colosse would be able to keep going, not so much because they had suppressed their human feelings, but because their relationship with God was what mattered most. 'I have learned in whatever state I am, to be content: I know how to be abased, and I know how to abound. Everywhere and in all things I have learned both to be full and to be hungry, both to abound and to suffer need. I can do all things through Christ who strengthens me' (Phil. 4:11-13).

A prayer for gratitude (1:12-14)

Paul also prayed that another consequence of their having been strengthened by God was that his readers would give **'thanks to the Father'** (1:12). He wanted them to become increasingly thankful. Two reasons stand out.

1. God had qualified them

In the first place, he wanted the Colossians to appreciate a thrilling truth — namely that God had **'qualified'** them to receive an **'inheritance'** (1:12). By describing salvation as something that believers inherit, the apostle was touching on a wonderful privilege that belongs to every Christian. God looks upon us as his children. Only a true son has the right to inherit what belongs to his father. The fact that Paul writes in this way tells us that he wanted the Christians in Colosse to be grateful to God because they really did have a stake in the wonderful future that God has promised to **'the saints'**, to each and every true believer.

Furthermore, this inheritance is **'in the light'** (1:12). **'Light'** here marks a contrast with the **'darkness'** of the believer's former life (1:13). It has a moral and a spiritual dimension. Believers are enlightened in the sense that they can now see things that were once obscure. The awful truth about personal sin and guilt and the glorious truth about Jesus Christ as the only Saviour of sinners have now been revealed with luminous clarity.

Paul's readers needed to understand that it was not that God had made their salvation a distant possibility. Though not in heaven yet, and though they could never have earned the privilege by their own efforts, they could anticipate it with complete confidence because their qualification did not depend on their own moral worth, but on the life and death of Jesus Christ as their substitute. This note of reassurance would be important to them. As we shall see, some of them might have gained the impression from the new teachers that they were actually 'disqualified' from a place among Christians of the first rank (see 2:18). In the same way, nervous believers are often fearful because they feel that they could never qualify for a place in God's favour. This is why the doctrine of justification by faith alone is so important. It reminds us that our right to a place in God's favour is not dependent on our performance in any way at all. It all hangs on what the Son of God has done in our place.

2. God had delivered them

In second place, in verse 13, Paul speaks of salvation as having been **'delivered'**. A dramatic rescue has taken place. Salvation involves being transferred from one kingdom to another. The Colossians had been transplanted from Satan's dominion, **'the power of darkness'**, to the **'kingdom of the Son of his love'** — that is to say, the kingdom that belongs to Jesus Christ, the beloved and only Son of God. This deliverance is explained in verse 14. It was achieved by none other than Jesus Christ himself. It involved **'redemption'**, the payment of a ransom at the cost of his own blood. The glorious outcome is **'the forgiveness of sins'**.

Again Paul is dealing in certainties. God had not done enough to make deliverance an outside possibility at some future date; he really had rescued those first-century Christians. The transfer was complete. They were not hovering between worlds. They had left one kingdom behind and had been placed firmly in another. People who have undergone this kind of experience have every reason to be profoundly grateful.

What about ourselves? Can we say that God has qualified us for heaven, so that our future there is guaranteed, and that he has rescued us from the clutches of a powerful tyrant and enlisted us in his service? Paul wanted every believer in Colosse to be thankful because God had qualified and delivered every single one of them.

Conclusion

Two things in particular stand out as we conclude our study of this passage.

Firstly, *Paul prayed for other Christians.* No doubt we do so too. But do we pray as he prayed, with resolutely spiritual priorities, crying out to God that our friends might achieve excellence in their walk with God? Paul prayed that God would endow his readers with an impressive combination of qualities, a large measure of 'spiritual understanding' (1:9), a life that was pleasing to God and increasingly filled with the knowledge of God's will (1:10). He also pleaded with God that they might be given the power to keep going and made truly grateful for a wonderful salvation (1:11-12).

Secondly, *Paul invites us to draw a conclusion.* 'Fulness' teaching, whatever form it takes, has a way of minimizing salvation. It leaves us with the strong impression that salvation is only a first step on the way to something more complete. Yet Paul speaks of salvation in glowing terms. It means that Jesus Christ has earned his people the right to an inheritance beyond compare. Because of him, our status has changed dramatically. We have been rescued from a desperate situation and transplanted into Christ's kingdom as redeemed and forgiven people. It is a terrible thing to imply that there is still something wanting after a salvation so marvellous and complete. No saved person should give the least hearing to anyone who would belittle it.

3.
The incomparable Christ

Please read Colossians 1:15-20

Suppose that someone you knew had recently become a Christian, but was disturbed and unhappy. Someone had suggested to your friend that his new-found faith in Christ was not enough. It was all very well as far as it went — certainly enough to guarantee the forgiveness of sins — but for a truly effective Christian life some additional blessing was needed. Your friend might have been told that he required something beyond what Christ could do, something that came from some other source. (Christians in first-century Colosse were being encouraged to seek the help of angels. Some modern believers are fixated with angels too. There is also a well-established line of thinking that we need the prayers of the saints.) Equally, your friend might have been told that he needed a further blessing which would come from Christ himself, as though the blessings of the Christian life come to us in stages — first conversion, then a deeper experience of 'fulness'. How would you help this person?

This was the apostle Paul's concern as he wrote the words we are considering in this chapter. The Christians in the town of Colosse to whom he was writing had been introduced to the gospel by a responsible evangelist named Epaphras, but their faith had been undermined by a group of newcomers with a subtly different emphasis. Paul's response, which forms the second part of a very long sentence that began in verse 9, was to explain the greatness of Christ. This is the best possible antidote for all Christians who are in danger of being sidetracked. Make much of Jesus, and lesser things will fade into the background. How could our faith be deficient if we place it in such a magnificent Saviour?

The result is sublime. A stupendous theme is explained in striking and dramatic prose. These few verses set a stern test for the preacher. The detail of the passage is extremely important. Each individual phrase has been chosen with particular care; each deserves attention. At the same time, it is also vital that we don't focus upon the detail to such a close degree that we lose sight of Paul's argument as it develops. We need a grasp of the total picture, an awareness of the cumulative effect of all of the apostle's statements taken together. His intention was to leave us in no doubt that Jesus is all that we could possibly ever want or need as a Saviour.

Christ the supreme Lord of all things (1:15-17)

Exactly who is Jesus? We can find the answer in these verses, although it is likely to swamp our senses. (It is very telling that the assertion **'he is'** is used so many times in this section. It has an insistent quality.)

1. The one who perfectly reveals God

First of all, we are told that Christ is **'the image of the invisible God'** (1:15). This takes us back to the story of the creation of man in Genesis 1:26. Every human being is made in God's image. Nevertheless, in this case, Paul had

something bigger in mind. He wanted his readers to understand that Christ resembles God to such a degree that there
is an exact match. We meet the same thought in Hebrews
1:3, where Jesus is described as the 'express image' of God
the Father. Just as a coin corresponds exactly to the die that
was stamped upon it, so the Lord Jesus Christ and God the
Father Almighty are completely alike in every respect.
Neither is the tiniest fraction more divine than the other.
Paul echoes the thought of John 1:18: 'No one has seen God
at any time. The only begotten Son, who is in the bosom of
the Father, he has declared him.' While God the Father
cannot be seen, those who have encountered Jesus need look
no further. 'God who commanded light to shine out of
darkness ... has shone in our hearts to give the light of the
knowledge of the glory of God in the face of Jesus Christ'
(2 Cor. 4:6). We cannot improve on Jesus' own words: 'He
who has seen me has seen the Father' (John 14:9). We can
catch the drift of Paul's argument at the outset. With a
Christ like this, how could we want or need more?

2. The heir of all things

Secondly, Paul describes our majestic Redeemer as **'the
firstborn over all creation'** (1:15). In the fourth century, a
group known as the Arians seized on this verse and claimed
that it meant that Jesus was merely the first being that God
created. They coined the slogan: 'There once was when he
was not.' Their modern counterparts, the Jehovah's Witnesses, use this verse in the same way. They have a considerable problem. This statement is surrounded by others that
demand that we accept that Jesus actually is Jehovah. We
cannot witness to Jehovah and undermine Jesus at the same
time. At this point Paul is in fact using the language of
inheritance and sonship. Just as a firstborn son is the rightful
heir to his father's property, all creation rightly belongs to

Christ. His Father made it and he has a rightful claim to it. Jesus not only owns each and every Christian by right of purchase; he owns the entire universe because he is the heir of all things.

3. The Creator of all things

In verse 16 Paul takes us a step further by saying of Jesus that **'By him all things were created.'** Nothing that exists was created by anyone else. 'All things were made through him, and without him nothing was made that was made' (John 1:3). This point is amplified by a series of statements. On the one hand, phrases like **'in heaven and ... on earth'** and **'visible and invisible'** are meant to be completely comprehensive. They are all-inclusive. Everything at all is embraced; nothing is left out.

On the other hand, it is likely that Paul had another element in mind. The new teachers in Colosse had a great deal to say about spiritual powers, those forces that are unseen by man but are real none the less. In every age, people tend to react to these hidden powers in one of two ways. Some people are drawn to them. They have a fascination for the supernatural. This is even true of a certain kind of Christian. There has recently been a spate of literature about encounters with angels. It clearly finds a ready sale. Over against this, others find that the idea of supernatural powers of any kind makes them uneasy. They feel very threatened by it all. The new teachers in Colosse had an appealing logic: the angels who never fell are noble beings, and we should try to recruit their assistance. By contrast, the angels who fell are very wicked, and we would do well to learn how to counteract them, or even placate them. Paul's response is clear-cut. By faith, we are joined to the Christ who made every one of them, in all their ranks and degrees. There is no need to be unduly overawed by the good angels, or to live in undue fear of the evil ones. They are created beings, answerable, as we are, to the God who made them.

Paul's overall point is given added emphasis at the close of verse 16. The Lord Christ was involved in the creation of all things, and all things were created for his glory and pleasure. His sovereignty is absolute. Nothing, not even Satan, falls outside the scope of his lordship.

Verse 17 opens with the statement: **'He is before all things.'** This can be rendered, 'He is the beginning.' He is the source, the origin, of the entire created order. 'In the beginning God created the heavens and the earth' (Gen. 1:1). This is not simply a statement about the timing of the event — namely that creation happened before anything else. It means that the eternal Son, who had existed from all eternity together with the Father, was the beginning from which the whole created universe sprang.

4. The one who sustains all things

Next we are told that **'In him all things consist'** (1:17). Not only did Christ create all that exists, but it only continues to exist because he is actively involved in holding it together. This begins at the most minute level of existence. Each oxygen atom has eight positively charged protons and eight neutrons with no charge. Charges of electricity and magnets operate according to Coulomb's law — namely that opposite poles or charges attract and like poles repel. If this same logic applied to the world of sub-atomic particles not one oxygen atom would hold together. Scientists talk about what they call a strong nuclear force, but they have no explanation for it. And the power that holds each atom together and controls the way that they combine in molecules makes the sap rise in every tree, keeps your heart beating, holds the soaring kestrel on top of its thermal and guides the wheeling constellations in their march across the heavens.

The believers in Colosse needed to stand in awe of the surpassing greatness of Christ, so, in words packed with significance, the apostle held him up before their astonished gaze. Are your senses reeling? And this magnificent, lordly, kingly Sovereign is your Saviour and Friend. If he is truly ours, what could possibly be missing?

Christ, the sufficient Saviour of the church (1:18-20)

1. The head of the church

As Paul develops his argument, the focus shifts from Christ as Creator to Christ as Redeemer. Nevertheless, Paul's logic is deeply satisfying. It is precisely because he is a mighty Lord that he is also **'head of the body, the church'** (1:18). Without the colossal power that called the worlds into being, he would not be able to save anyone at all. Equally, our salvation is not in the hands of someone who is quite powerful, but the one who has *all* power in heaven and also on this fractious and rebellious earth. In the ancient world the gods of Greece and Rome were rather like the comic-book superheroes of the present day. They were reputed to be more powerful than their human devotees. They had abilities that were supernatural. Even so, there were limits to the powers possessed by these entities. Jesus, by contrast, has power without limit.

The apostle also uses this metaphor of head and body in Ephesians 5:23, but here his main concern is to point out that Christ is indispensable. Without a head a body cannot function. There will be no sight, hearing, thought processes, intelligence, or direction. In the same way, without its head the church is at best a lifeless corpse. It is not that Jesus is a valuable addition, a useful acquisition; without him the church cannot be. Without him all is lost. To be without

Christ is to be completely without hope. No worse fate is possible.

2. The one who is exalted to the highest place

In describing our Saviour as **'the beginning, the firstborn from the dead'** (1:18), the apostle indicates that Christ is the first of a new humanity. We who expect to rise into the life of God owe it all to him because he has risen for us. But although we benefit from his glorious resurrection, it was not solely for our benefit. The stupendous majesty of creation, the wonderful grace of redemption, has a single aim in view: **'that in all things he may have the pre-eminence'** (1:18). His place at the highest summit is unchallenged. He is exalted far above all. Is there a hint here that the new teachers were claiming a degree of eminence for themselves, as though they deserved some recognition for their role as intermediaries with the unseen world? It is always a temptation for Christian leaders to want a place in the sun, but the primacy belongs to Jesus. The church has but one head for the simple reason that he far overtops any possible rivals. There is no scope whatever for popes in the Christian world. This even applies to Protestant 'popes', those empire-builders who treat local churches as small ponds where they can be the biggest fish. A good test for a church or an individual Christian is to ask who sits enthroned in glory in their mental world.

3. The one in whom all the fulness of the Godhead dwells

There is a translation issue in verse 19. The debate focuses on the fact that someone was **'pleased'** that **'all the fulness'** had taken up residence in Christ. But who was pleased? English translations of the Bible and evangelical commentators have arrived at different conclusions. There are good reasons for thinking that it should read, 'In him all the fulness of God was pleased to dwell'.[1] It is sometimes argued that an abstraction like a 'fulness' cannot take pleasure in anything, but a comparison with 2:9 makes it clear that, in this case, 'all the fulness of the Godhead' has made its home in the person of God's Son.

Paul's reason for introducing this topic was pastoral. He was concerned for the believers in Colosse, whose enjoyment of their faith had been undermined because it was being suggested that they did not yet have the spiritual fulness that might be theirs if only they could move on from the point where Epaphras had left them. The new teachers had told them that there was something beyond what the normal Christian experienced in Christ alone, that there were new depths to be plumbed. Paul set out to allay their fears that this might actually be true by pointing out that all the fulness of the divine nature is joyously present in Jesus Christ. It follows that anyone who has a share in Christ has all that there is of God. Christ is inexhaustible. The treasures of divinity will never run out; the supply of grace is limitless. If we are joined by faith to him, everything that exists in God becomes accessible to us. All his attributes, in all their boundless perfection, are ours to rest in and enjoy. His searing holiness, his love that knows no limit, his immeasurable power — when Christ makes his home in a human heart he brings all these and more with him. While we may not yet know God as we ought, or appreciate and enjoy him to the degree that could be ours, it remains true that the God that we do know, enjoy and appreciate is completely and wholly ours in Christ. We have far more in Christ than we have yet begun to realize.

4. The one who reconciles all things to God

In verse 20 it becomes clear that, having taken up residence in Christ, all the fulness of Godhead has been active in reconciliation. God in Christ is the great reconciler. This reconciliation has a cosmic dimension. It involves **'all things ... whether things on earth or things in heaven'**. Because of human sin, the entire universe is out of joint. By introducing the word **'reconcile'**, Paul has given us a brutal reminder that there is something seriously at fault with the human race. Our needs, especially on the physical and material level, are many, but over-arching them all is our urgent need to be made right with God, the God whom we have offended by our foolishness and sin. At the same time, reconciliation is gloriously available and it has its origin in the mind of God. All the initiative is his. There is only one source of reconciliation, the fulness of Godhead in Christ. There is no point looking for it anywhere else. The scope of this reconciliation is colossal. Just as the problem extends far beyond the human race, it is not merely human beings who are to be put right with God. Creation itself was affected by the Fall and the broken universe is to be restored. Even so, some of that restoration will have the character of a pacification. Writing to the Christians in Philippi, Paul speaks of a time when, 'at the name of Jesus every knee should bow, of those in heaven, and of those on earth, and of those under the earth, and that every tongue should confess that Jesus Christ is Lord, to the glory of God the Father' (Phil. 2:10-11). Every knee will bow because some will have been won round and others will be forced to submit.

Paul ends this section by noting that while reconciliation is a thrilling possibility, it is far from cheap or easy. Peace between God and man and between a ruined cosmos and its Maker is only available because of the sufferings of Christ.

Reconciliation has come about **'through the blood of his cross'**. It cannot be achieved in any other way.

Conclusion

The scenario that I outlined in the opening paragraph of this chapter is not far-fetched. Even today, Christians are sometimes given the impression that although they might have Christ for their Saviour, some vital added extra is missing. Something more is needed. Paul's response to this line of reasoning is to elaborate on the greatness and splendour of Christ. This leaves us with an inescapable conclusion. The Lord of glory is himself so wonderful that to insist that people need more than Christ is absurd. He cannot be excelled or surpassed. Do we realize how much we have in him? Every true Christian has been linked, with chains that cannot be broken, to the most wonderful person of them all, someone who represents God to mankind to the fullest and most complete degree, someone who not only existed prior to the creation of all things, but who participated in their creation. He is the head of the church, the first of a new humanity and the one in whom God is present to the utmost extent. All true Christians long to know the Christ they have with greater intensity and consistency, but he cannot be improved upon. To inform people that they need to move on from what they have in Christ is to insult him.

This passage closes by touching on our greatest need as human beings. For those who have failed to meet the standard that God has set, reconciliation is an urgent necessity. Is God willing to be at peace with us? No reader of this book need spend a day longer in uncertainty. Blood has been shed; a penalty has been paid and, for all who come in faith to Jesus Christ, our moral and spiritual debts have been cancelled. But, in view of all that we have learned about the identity of the great reconciler, the position of the merest beginner in Christian things is breathtaking. Who was it that bled for first-century believers in Colosse and twenty-first century Christians throughout the world? The Creator bled and suffered; the Lord of all things was bruised; the King of angels was spat upon; the one who controls the surging tides and the march of the seasons was nailed to a cross. Can such a sacrifice, from such a person, ever be improved upon? We don't know how the Colossians received this letter, but we can gauge our own reaction. Presented with such a Christ, the pearl of great price, should we hanker for more than we have in him, or be amazed at what we have?

4.
An incomparable salvation

Please read Colossians 1:21-23

Paul has concluded his hymn of praise to Christ (1:15-20), an extended treatment of the greatness of the Christian's Saviour. In that section we discovered that Jesus is supreme, that he is exalted far above all things. We also saw that he is sufficient. He is all that we need as a Saviour, for he is well able to save all his people to the utmost degree. His power to save is limitless. No case of human need, however desperate, is beyond him.

Now Paul moves on from considering who Christ is, the splendour of his being and the endless resources of his sovereign mercy, to look instead at what Christ has done for his people. This was enormously relevant to his original readers. The church in Colosse was troubled by a new breed of teachers offering a form of spirituality that posed a subtle threat to their spiritual well-being. These men were careful not to say anything that belittled the Lord Jesus Christ and his achievement directly, but Paul could see that this would be an inevitable consequence of their teaching. By insisting that the believer should look beyond mere salvation for an experience of 'fulness', the new teachers hinted that what Christ has done for us is only effective up to a point. We need something more to make our Christian experience complete. Paul's response in these verses is just as relevant to believers today, because the Colossian syndrome has not gone away. It has been repackaged in a variety of ways, but believers are still being enticed with the notion that salvation is only a beginning. We must move on to greater things, we are told. In the end, if all we have is Christ and his salvation, something is missing.

In the previous section Paul's response was to make much of Christ himself. How can a person who is united to such a complete and excellent Saviour be lacking something vital? Now, in this new section, Paul makes much of salvation; he emphasizes the greatness of it. Far from being a necessary but relatively minor prelude to a blessing that would surpass it, the salvation of a soul is an experience entirely without parallel. The change that has come over every believer cannot be minimized. No greater experience is possible in this life.

What believers were (1:21)

Paul begins his treatment of salvation by explaining why we need to be saved. He does so by giving a graphic and hard-hitting description of the human condition. This is how things once stood for every Christian, whether in Colosse in the first century, or all over the world today. It is also a telling and forthright picture of every person who has yet to be reconciled to God. You may even be surprised to recognize yourself in these words. If so, your situation is alarming. Don't rest for a moment until this description belongs firmly in your past.

1. Alienated from God

The apostle begins by saying that there had been a time when the Colossians had been **'alienated'**. The idea is that of estrangement. At one time 'alienation' was part of the vocabulary of the political left. Karl Marx had concluded that capitalist exploitation had left the workers of all lands disaffected with their lot, at odds with the world at large and with one another. Marx was not entirely wrong. He had shrewdly noticed a genuine problem, but had failed to diagnose the root cause. Paul would have us understand that the heart of the problem is alienation from God. We enter this world estranged from our Maker. That critical relationship, on which all our other relationships depend, has become fractured. Because there is a breach between mankind and God, we find it difficult to be at peace in any area of our lives. We lead lonely lives in an unfriendly universe, cut off from each other and from nature.

2. Hostile towards God

This situation has come about because human beings have a deep-seated attitude problem. The phrase, **'enemies in your mind'**, is a hard-hitting way of saying that at the heart of each one of us there is an inbred hostility to God. From the moment we leave the womb we are God-haters. Christian communicators in the secularized West often refer to a prevailing mood of apathy. While this is an understandable reaction to a complete lack of interest in Christianity and a bored refusal to take it seriously, the real problem is not apathy at all. Apathy is merely an attempt to dress intense dislike in polite garb. Just occasionally the mask slips and the underlying sullenness and aggression are briefly visible.

This basic enmity results in behaviour that is displeasing to God, **'wicked works'**. At this point Paul echoes the teaching of Jesus himself: 'Those things which proceed out of the mouth come from the heart, and they defile a man. For out of the heart proceed evil thoughts, murders, adulteries, fornications, thefts, false witness, blasphemies' (Matt. 15:18-19). Our actions are shaped by deep-rooted drives and motives that all express this sense of enmity against God. If it had been within our power, we would have torn him from the throne of the universe and sat upon it ourselves. In short, unless and until we are changed by the grace of God, things could hardly be worse.

What believers have become (1:21-22)

1. Reconciled to God

When a person becomes a Christian, he or she undergoes a dramatic transformation. Paul explains in these verses that those who were once engaged in active hostilities against God are now his friends. The warring parties have been **'reconciled'** (1:21). The word translated 'reconciled' here is more intense than the normal Greek term. Paul added a prefix to it, which has the effect of making the term stronger. It speaks of total and utter reconciliation, reconciliation without a doubt. The quarrel has been resolved so completely that no question marks remain.

How was this startling transformation achieved? Paul leaves us in no doubt that Jesus brought reconciliation about **'in the body of his flesh, through death'** (1:22). This direct, almost earthy, language insists that Christ acquired a human body at his incarnation and in that very body died a man's death for the sake of his people. Paul's matter-of-fact insistence on Christ's human flesh and 'the blood of his cross' (1:20) was probably intended to counter an idea that was beginning to gain ground in the Greek-speaking world of the eastern Mediterranean. This was the idea that spirit is good and matter is evil. No true god would stoop to take a body of flesh and blood because, in doing so, its divinity would become tainted. In due course, this kind of thinking became one of the main features of a loose group of movements collectively described as 'Gnosticism'.

2. Justified before God

In the face of this kind of thinking, Paul left his readers in no doubt that reconciliation between an offended God and rebellious human beings could not take place unless God the Son became man in order to suffer in his own person the penalty that human sin had earned. This was the only way to remove the offence and make sinners acceptable to God, to present them **'holy, and blameless, and above reproach in his sight'** (1:22). The word **'present'** has echoes of the law courts, as though the defendant is being paraded before the judge in full confidence that the verdict will go in his favour.

At this point Paul chose three synonymous expressions, **'holy'**, **'blameless'** and **'above reproach'**, to give added weight to his message. The repetition rams the point home. The most demanding and exacting judge in the universe is completely satisfied with the credentials of those who stand before him. He now sees no fault at all in those who were once his sworn foes, and this is all and only because Jesus has taken all the blame for all the sins of all his people.

The contrast between past and present could not be more marked. In our former state, things could hardly be worse. We were 'without Christ' and therefore had 'no hope' and were 'without God in the world' (Eph. 2:12). Now, however, things could hardly be better. Because Christ has died in our place, God has no reason at all to reject us and every reason to embrace us as friends.

This was exciting news for the Christians in Colosse and should come as a profound relief to believers today who have been tempted to yield to modern versions of the Colossian syndrome. 'Fulness' teaching, in its various forms, is potentially dangerous because it subtly downgrades conversion by suggesting that it is only one of two experiences that we need to go through, and the second of those experiences is the one that makes all the difference. It says, in effect, 'Yes, it is a good thing to be saved, but salvation by itself will leave you incomplete.' But what could be greater than the momentous transformation described here? To go from enmity to acceptance, from hostility to friendship, from frosty suspicion on our part and wrath and indignation on God's part to a completely new footing where mutual love is the keynote, is surely the most enormous change possible. Any converted person has received a blessing of colossal proportions. The new teachers in Colosse had subtly tried not only to diminish Christ but also to chip away at his people's appreciation of what he had done for them; yet what more can Almighty love do than to turn a congenital rebel into a delighted worshipper and valued companion? The only fit response to such royal generosity is amazement and gratitude. Are you both amazed and grateful?

What believers must continue to be (1:23)

Given that conversion to Christ involves a cataclysmic change of enormous dimensions in everyone who undergoes it, what is the real test that a person has truly undergone this far-reaching transformation?

1. They persevere

The litmus test is perseverance. True conversion is a lasting change. Those who do not stay the course have a question mark hanging over them. If we say, 'Jesus has saved me,' we have a point to prove. This explains Paul's phrase, **'if indeed you continue in the faith, grounded and steadfast...'**

It is important that we do not jump to a false conclusion at this point, as though Paul were suggesting that it is actually possible for a genuine Christian to deny the faith completely at some point after conversion. In Romans 8:29-30 we find him teaching that nothing is more secure than a person who has experienced the love of God. Such people are the objects of God's loving choice in eternity past; he appointed their eternal destiny not only before they were born, but before the world was made. At some point in their own lifetime each of them heard God calling them to his side in a way that over- came all their doubts, fears and selfishness. In due course, even though they had sinned against him, they received the 'not guilty' verdict from the Judge of all the earth which meant that they were justified. Paul's logic is that no one whom God has foreknown, predestined, called and justified will not also be glorified. As the apostle Peter put it, a wonderful inheritance has been reserved for all believers and they are being 'kept by the power of God' for that same inheritance (1 Peter 1:4-5).

At the same time, those who are being kept by God recognize that they have a duty to persevere, and that is what Paul has in mind in verse 23. While no true Christian is ever lost, there are some unhappy souls who give the impression of having come to faith in Christ, but with the passage of time this impression proves to be ill-founded. Paul urged steadfastness upon his friends so that there would be no doubt that God was keeping them by his grace.

2. They abide in Christ

We need to grasp that Paul is not simply advocating steadfastness in general terms. His focus here is upon continuing
in Christ, the same Christ who is described in such sublime
language in verses 15-20: '… the image of the invisible God,
the firstborn over all creation. For by him all things were
created that are in heaven and that are on earth, visible and
invisible, whether thrones or dominions or principalities or
powers. All things were created through him and for him.
And he is before all things, and in him all things consist. And
he is the head of the body, the church, who is the beginning,
the firstborn from the dead, that in all things he may have the
pre-eminence. For it pleased the Father that in him all the
fulness should dwell, and by him to reconcile all things to
himself, by him, whether things on earth or things in heaven,
having made peace through the blood of his cross.' We are to
continue in the faith that unites us to him. We are to remain
grounded and settled in this glorious Christ.

The same idea is stated in the opposite way later in the
verse. We are not to be **'moved away from the hope of the
gospel'**. There is to be no slippage. Christians must not lose
their moorings like a boat that has drifted away from a safe
anchorage. For the Colossians this would mean being
attracted to something less than the gospel they had embraced at the outset, the gospel that had brought such a great
salvation to them.

3. They have a sure hope

The word **'hope'** here does not have any speculative overtones, as it does in modern English. In the early part of 2005
many of the inhabitants of my native city were saying to
themselves, 'Will Sunderland get promotion this season? I
hope so.'[1] I can use the word 'hope' in that context without

any real expectation that my hopes will come true. In modern English usage, hopes can be misplaced. Paul, however, intended 'hope' to mean confidence. After all, ours is a gospel that engenders confidence. The Colossians needed to recover their sense of certainty and conviction.

This is why Paul emphasized that the gospel that they had heard was the same gospel that had been the means of transforming others in other places too. (It has never been literally true that the gospel has been preached to **'every creature under heaven'**, not even two thousand years on from Paul's day. It was however, certainly the case that, in the Roman world at least, virtually every sizeable centre of population already had a Christian community.) The Colossians had not heard a defective gospel, something less than the full gospel, because in responding to Epaphras' message they had responded to the very same gospel that Paul preached. The imperative, then, was not to move on to something new and different, but to remain fixed on the ground that they had occupied since first coming to Christ.

Conclusion

In seeking to reassure the believers in Colosse that what Christ had done for them in saving them was a blessing beyond compare, Paul gave them in passing a working definition of what it is to be a Christian. A Christian was once God's enemy. He has been reconciled to God and owes this transformation entirely to Jesus Christ. He is under a tremendous obligation to go on, not to new things, but to go on entrusting himself to the Christ whom he first trusted at the outset. The Christian life begins with faith in Christ; it continues with faith in Christ all the way to the gate of heaven. It never moves beyond, or away from, faith in Christ. Where do you fit into this pattern of things?

5.
Paul describes the nature of his ministry

Please read Colossians 1:24-29

These verses form part of a larger section, which continues as far as Colossians 2:7. This section has a distinctly personal tone. In verses 24-29, the pronoun 'I' occurs three times and 'me' occurs twice. Ordinarily, the apostle Paul was reluctant to write about himself and his ministry. He made a deliberate attempt to avoid self-promotion and to focus instead upon Christ (see 2 Cor. 4:5). It seems, however, that the nature of true Christian leadership had become an issue in Colosse. The church there had given a hearing to a group of men who seemed very plausible. Paul's warning in 2:4, 'lest anyone should deceive you with persuasive words', suggests that the church had been taken in and drawn away, to some extent, from the teachings of the evangelist who had founded the church. With this in mind, Paul outlined something of the character of his own service to God and, in effect, invited a comparison. Who resembled the apostle most — the newcomers, with all their showmanship, or Epaphras, who had first preached the gospel to them?

Paul rejoices in his sufferings (1:24)

It is not surprising that Paul should refer to his **'sufferings'**. When he wrote these words, he was under house arrest in Rome. There has been much debate, however, about the phrase in the middle of the verse where Paul speaks of filling up in his own flesh **'what is lacking in the afflictions of Christ'**.

1. What he did not mean

First of all, we can be clear that this is not a reference to the redemptive sufferings of Christ. In all his writings, Paul does not use the word 'afflictions' in connection with the atonement that Christ purchased for his people. Instead he refers to our Saviour's 'cross', his 'blood', his 'death', and so on. There is no suggestion here that Christ has not suffered enough to pay the full penalty for our sins, or that it is incumbent on us to add some sufferings of our own until the full price is paid. (This is the thinking that lies behind the Roman Catholic teaching of purgatory.) This view is actually highly insulting to our Saviour and to all that he achieved by suffering in the place of his people.

2. Suffering that precedes the coming of the Messiah

In that case, what did Paul mean by **'the afflictions of Christ'**? It is likely that there are two levels of meaning here.

To begin with, the apostle's phrase has echoes of an expression in common use among Jewish scholars at that time, the 'woes of the Messiah' or 'tribulations of the Messiah'. It was widely supposed that the coming of the Messiah would be preceded by a time of intense trial. ('Woes' or 'tribulations' also had the sense of 'birth pangs'.) This would not have seemed at all strange to the first Christians, who would have remembered Jesus' words: 'For then there will be great tribulation, such as has not been since the beginning of the world until this time, no, nor ever shall be' (Matt. 24:21). The main difference was that, while Jews did not know the identity of the Messiah, Christians identified this tribulation as something that would precede the Second Coming of Christ.

If this view is correct we should think of 'the afflictions of Christ' not so much as afflictions that he suffered, but as afflictions that would come upon the church prior to his return. This would help to explain why the apostle told the believers in Colosse that his sufferings were for them and **'for the sake of [Christ's] body, which is the church'**. He could **'rejoice'** because his imprisonment, and for that matter his many other trials, meant that he was 'filling up' in his flesh, or receiving in his body, sufferings that would otherwise come the way of believers in Colosse and elsewhere.

3. The unity between Christ and his people

A second possibility that deserves to be considered is connected with the organic unity that exists between Christ and his people. On the road to Damascus, Paul made the alarming discovery that the risen Christ identified so closely with believers that to persecute them was to persecute him (Acts 9:4). Satan would like to make the Lord Christ suffer, but cannot get at him. Since his resurrection and ascension Jesus has been out of reach of the Evil One. The devil therefore targets instead those who are united to Christ. The servants of God suffer because they have an organic connection with their Master. They are so closely identified with him that the enemy tries to inflict damage on Christ by harming his people. In Paul's case, suffering was something that he expected from the outset. Soon after his conversion, God sent Ananias to help Paul recover his sight with these words:

'I will show him how many things he must suffer for my name's sake' (Acts 9:16). The former persecutor was now to be among the persecuted. In this case, his 'rejoicing', though the suffering itself was far from pleasant, arose from the fact that it was a guarantee that Paul's ministry was authentic.

How did the new teachers in Colosse compare in this regard? Certainly when Paul measured himself against his rivals in Corinth he challenged them to prove their genuineness by asking whether they had suffered to the same extent that he had: 'Are they ministers of Christ? — I speak as a fool — I am more: in labours more abundant, in stripes above measure, in prisons more frequently, in deaths often' (2 Cor. 11:23).

How are we to understand the principle that Paul lays down with respect to the world of evangelical churches in the West today? Few of us have suffered in any marked way for the cause of Christ. Perhaps the critical test is that the one who has been proved faithful in small things will stand much sterner tests, should they come along. And while our leaders may not be called upon to be martyrs, some of the lesser trials are real enough — relative poverty, misrepresentation, isolation and the ostracism of the wider religious community.

Paul, a steward of the mystery (1:25-27)

Paul closed the previous section of his argument by describing himself as a minister of the gospel (1:23). Now he refers to himself as a minister of the church (1:24-25). As we have already noted, the word **'minister'** here does not describe an occupation. It is not a professional title. It means 'servant'. The true Christian leader is called not to a life in the limelight, milking the esteem of an admiring public, but to a life of service. His service has two aspects. He is to serve both the Word of God and the people of God. These two go together; they are inextricably linked. The true spiritual leader will serve God's people best by teaching them the Word of God.

In the modern world, we can sometimes observe clerical persons with very different agendas from the one that Paul and Epaphras both embraced. Some are sacramentalists. They try to serve Christian people by making rites and ceremonies available to them. Others work hard to meet the material and social needs of people who suffer all kinds of deprivation. While such work is extremely valuable, genuine spiritual leadership must have another focus altogether. Its aim is to **'present every man perfect in Christ Jesus'** (1:28) — that is, to bring Christian people to well-rounded maturity. The only way this can be achieved is to bring the Word of God to bear on their minds, hearts, wills and consciences. Try to get to know God better without getting to know the Bible better, and you will fail miserably. This should also leave us in no doubt that every generation has a crying need for the kind of people that Paul had in mind, those who can serve the churches because they are responsible servants of God's revealed truth.

1. The responsibilities of a steward

Paul described his ministry as a **'stewardship from God'** (1:25). The dominant idea here is that a 'steward' is someone with a commission from a superior, someone who has been required to discharge a trust. Essentially a steward looks after the property of another. In this case, the apostle had been entrusted with the gospel. He exercised his stewardship faithfully when that message was conveyed to others. (This is in keeping with his statement that the 'stewardship' was **'given'** to him for the Colossians. We meet the same logic in the parallel passage in Ephesians 3:8: 'To me, who am less than the least of all the saints, this grace was given, that I should preach among the Gentiles the unsearchable riches of Christ.')

As a responsible steward he was required to **'fulfil the word of God'** (1:25). The word **'fulfil'** actually translates the same Greek verb that Paul used when he spoke of filling up in his flesh 'the afflictions of Christ' (1:24). It means that he was to carry out his commission fully and completely. We ought to note at this point that this involved more than the apostle 'doing his best'. The **'word of God'** is fulfilled when the power of God is at work through his human instruments and the promise in Isaiah's prophecy comes true:

> So shall my word be that goes forth from my mouth;
> It shall not return to me void,
> But it shall accomplish what I please,
> And it shall prosper in the thing for which I sent it
> (Isa. 55:11).

2. What Paul meant by the 'mystery'

In order to discharge his duty and pass on the message that God had entrusted to him, Paul had to convey what he describes as **'the mystery'** (1:26). In using this word, he was giving a distinctly Christian meaning to a term that was part of the jargon that was probably employed by the new teachers. It was certainly in common use in the wider religious scene around the eastern Mediterranean during the first century. It usually conveyed the idea of initiation into a special secret. For that reason, it smacked of elitism. For the most part, the idea of being initiated into 'the mysteries' was something that first-century people encountered in the wide variety of pagan cults that existed at the time.

No doubt the new teachers in Colosse were shrewd enough to put a Christian veneer on this mentality. They would employ Christian terminology to convince those who took their emphasis on board that they were being admitted to the 'inner ring', the special circle of devotees who had experienced a level of blessedness that the normal Christian could not expect.

By contrast, Paul had something quite different in mind. He used 'mystery' in the same way that we use the word 'revelation'. His thinking was as follows. There is something vital that human beings desperately need to know for their eternal well-being but it is hidden from them. They could never discover it for themselves. This, of course, is the gospel, with all that it has to say about the desperate plight of humankind and God's generous grace in providing a Saviour. The wonderful reality is that God has taken the initiative. What we could never have found out for ourselves, for all our frantic efforts, God has revealed. A glorious message of truth that was once **'hidden from ages and from generations'** (think of the long centuries while the truth of God was completely unknown across the overwhelming bulk of our planet) he has now **'revealed to his saints'** (1:26).

In passing, we should note that **'saints'** is a term that means 'holy ones'. As such, it does not refer to especially distinguished Christians, but to all the people of God. In Colosse it was being suggested that there was a privileged inner circle who had received revelations denied to others. Paul's emphasis, however, is that the gospel, once unknown to mankind at large, has now been revealed to all believers, whoever and wherever they are. This is even more explicit in Ephesians 3:4-6, where it is made clear that the gospel is as much for Gentiles as for Jews. Paul writes of 'the mystery of Christ, which in other ages was not made known to the sons of men, as it has now been revealed by the Spirit to his holy apostles and prophets: that the Gentiles should be fellow heirs, of the same body, and partakers of his promise in Christ through the gospel'.

Paul writes of 'the mystery' in extravagant terms in verse 27. God has **'willed to make known'** (and it was therefore Paul's commission to pass on) **'the riches of the glory of this mystery'**. 'Glory' translates a Greek word that includes the idea of intense brightness with that of crushing weight. The glory of God is such that sinful mortals cannot look upon it; the sight would be too much for them to bear. It is also so overwhelming that it falls upon us and leaves us prostrate. Here 'glory' is combined with the idea of **'riches'**, in particular with extreme wealth. The heart of this glorious message is Christ himself (1:28). The Christian leader is not merely to expound Scripture; he is to preach Christ. (There is a way of talking about the Bible which can end up obscuring Christ. With some preachers, Jesus gets hidden behind a forest of words and arguments.)

At heart then, the difference between Paul and the new teachers in Colosse was that he preached Christ, while their preaching mentioned Christ but subtly undermined him. We can see what Paul understood by preaching Christ from the glorious description of our Saviour in verses 15-20. The apostle held up before people a majestic Saviour in all his fulness, with all his glorious perfections on display. This was not the diminished, shrivelled, pygmy Jesus of much con-temporary preaching. Moreover, we cannot preach Christ without preaching the Scriptures. The only Christ who can save us from our sins is the one revealed in the Bible. Preaching Christ, whether to first-century Colossians or to modern people in all their enormous variety, involves more than stating objective facts about the Son of God. Note that Paul refers to **'Christ in you, the hope of glory'** (1:27). The gospel is about a Christ who can be experienced and known, who takes up residence within the believer and who is not only glorious in himself, but brings with him the **'hope'** — that is to say, the confident certainty — of glory for all who are united to him.

Paul, a diligent servant (1:28-29)

1. The minister as a servant of God's people

The best way we can serve the people of God is to do as Paul did and explain his message to them. This will involve a negative aspect, **'warning every man'** (1:28), just as the apostle does in this very letter. This is not an easy or a popular task. In today's world, exposing dangerous teachings will get you a name for being unloving and judgemental. They probably said the same things about Paul! It also has a positive thrust, **'teaching every man'** (1:28).

Incidentally, the repeated phrase, **'every man'**, tells us that Paul was concerned at the elitist tendencies of the new teaching in Colosse. No one was to be excluded. All without exception were to be warned, every individual in particular was to be taught. It also suggests that Paul gave himself to dealing with people on an individual level as well as teaching when churches were assembled together.

To sum up so far, the authentic Christian leader is to be a humble servant of God's people. His service will take the form of explaining all that God has revealed patiently and thoroughly, and always with the focus on Christ himself. When the time comes for any local church to call a new pastor, it cannot afford to be satisfied with anything less than a man who will make that his life's work among them.

2. The ministry is hard work

Another mark of the calibre of a true Christian leader is his capacity for work (1:29). The Greek word translated **'labour'** means working to the point of exhaustion. **'Striving'** translates a word taken from the world of athletics. It describes the wholehearted commitment of the sportsman who gives his all. Our verb 'agonize' is taken from the same Greek word.

There is a clear link here between our working and **'his working'**. The way for us to experience God's power is not to employ some mystic technique, but to attempt something for God and find in the doing of it that he gives the power that we need. You will never find out just what great things God can do in a human life until you try something. What does it feel like when God is doing great things? It feels like hard work. How do we know that God is at work in the world? Look at his servants. If they are hard at it, we know that he is working in and through them. If, on the other hand, a pastor treats his study as a lounge, his pulpit will be a disgrace.

Conclusion

Paul could see that his friend and colleague Epaphras had suffered because the newcomers in Colosse had promoted themselves in a way that belittled him. The challenge that faced the members of the church there is one that faces believers in the West today. We are confronted with competing views of the true nature of Christian leadership.

Paul made it clear that he stood with Epaphras. In doing so he demonstrated that he had a very high view of his calling. This is apparent in his view of himself. He was the servant of God's people and a servant of God, a steward entrusted with something precious beyond words, a message that he had to transmit faithfully and completely. His commission required him to serve not just an elite handful, but all the people of God, and to do so to the point of exhaustion.

Modern Christians need to ask themselves where they stand on this matter. Do we place ourselves under the authority of men who are willing to serve the people of God, or their own interests; men who preach Christ, or themselves; men who are willing to pay a price for the privilege of their calling, or those who feel cheated without recognition and comfort?

6.
Paul identifies with his readers

Please read Colossians 2:1-5

In this section, Paul continues the defence of himself and his
ministry that he began in 1:24. This had become necessary
because new teachers had gained themselves a hearing in the
church at Colosse and their approach to leadership was very
different from the one that Paul himself had embraced, and
also from the approach taken by the founder of the church,
Epaphras.

Paul's response to the challenge posed by the newcomers
should strike a chord with modern Christians too. There are
many fault lines in the modern evangelical scene. Christians
divide over doctrinal issues, such as the sovereignty of God
in salvation, the true nature and significance of Christian
baptism, spiritual gifts, church government, the style of
worship, and many more. It is also apparent that the kind of
division that Paul was addressing in this epistle is still with
us, in that some Christian leaders appear to resemble the
newcomers in Colosse, whereas others model themselves,
however ineffectively, on Paul and Epaphras. In the verses
we have now reached in our study, there is a slight shift in
emphasis as Paul explained his hopes for his readers and the
reasons that prompted him to become involved in the situation that was developing in Colosse.

Paul's ambition for his readers (2:1-3)

As this section begins, Paul describes himself as being
involved in a **'conflict'** (2:1) on behalf of his original readers.
As we have seen earlier, these were the members of the
church in Colosse, a town in the Lycus Valley in Asia Minor,
some distance inland from Ephesus. Paul also mentioned
'those in Laodicea' and went on to add a reference to all
those who had not seen his face **'in the flesh'**. At this point,
Paul was probably thinking of the believers in the nearby
town of Hierapolis. The three towns were situated close to
one another, were in easy reach of each other and were easily
lumped together in the minds of people who lived in that
region. The churches in each of the three towns had all been
founded by the same evangelist, Epaphras, and were close
enough for a considerable degree of mutual contact to have
been likely. This closeness also made it likely that each
church had been affected to some degree by the new teachers.

Even though Paul had not been to any of the churches in
person, he felt that he could not stand idly by as battle lines
were drawn. The **'conflict'** was very intense. (Paul used the
Greek word from which we get our word 'agony'.) In es-
sence, it was a battle for the souls and the future of the
churches. What would the churches of the Lycus Valley be
like half a century after Paul wrote these words? What would
be the 'flavour', or 'ethos', of those churches, and what kind
of leaders would they throw up? Would they still stand
where they had originally stood? Looking on from a distance
of twenty centuries, many older Christians in the West today
might find this all very poignant, since they will know of
churches that have been effectively captured for a very
different brand of Christianity from the one they embraced at
first.

In Colosse and the neighbouring towns, the combatants
were initially the new teachers on the one hand and Epaphras

on the other, but once Paul heard what Epaphras was up against, he could not stand on the sidelines. The newcomers were trying to win the members of the three churches over to their cause. Paul was concerned to prevent this because he feared that it would entail long-term damage, with the churches being seduced away, not only from a certain style of Christianity, but in due course from the gospel itself. The same battle is going on in church after church today.

The future of the three churches would be secure if they could turn out the kind of Christians who would not be easily swayed by the agenda of the new teachers. With this in mind, Paul hoped that his letter would build up the believers in each of three related areas.

1. He wanted to encourage them

First of all, he was concerned **'that their hearts may be encouraged'** (2:2). By their **'hearts'** he meant the innermost core of their being, the very centre and focus of what made them the people they were. The word translated **'encouraged'** was once used in secular Greek to describe what could happen in wartime if a regiment had become thoroughly dispirited, to the point where it had turned out to be unreliable and a doubtful asset in battle. Believers can be like that, sometimes losing all stomach for the fight. A situation that was potentially alarming could be transformed if a senior general came alongside the regiment and took the situation in hand, putting new heart into the dejected soldiers. In the same way, since Paul was under house arrest and could not come alongside the Colossian believers in person, he prayed that his letter might have the same effect, helping to stiffen the spiritual resolve of people whose vitality had been undermined. Paul wrote as he did because he sensed one of the dangers that occur when spiritual leaders flirt with novel teachings. Error has a dispiriting effect on Christians. When church members feel that their leaders are calling vital truths into question, they become anxious and inward-looking. Courage is sapped and vitality is diluted.

2. He wanted them to be united

Secondly, Paul wanted their hearts to be **'knit together in love'** (2:2). Again, he used a very strong term. The verb translated **'knit'** can also be rendered as 'welded'. This suggests that he envisaged an extremely strong bond. Paul clearly saw another danger threatening the church at Colosse. Error is divisive. It sets brother against brother. It introduces an element of uncertainty into relationships because, as each Christian looks at his fellow believers, he is now fearful where he was once confident: 'I cannot be certain where he stands any more.'

The irony of our present situation is that many modern believers have exactly the opposite perception to Paul. There is a widespread belief that doctrine divides. As a result, in some circles, there is an unspoken agreement that teaching should be kept to a minimum so as not to split the church. If a local church, however, is to be more than a club linking people with a shared set of tastes, it must unite around a shared set of convictions about Christ and his gospel. A much more common scenario than doctrine dividing a church is what happens when new teachings take hold in a local fellowship and some believers are left with the uneasy feeling that, while they have stayed where they were, their church has moved away from them. Unity in love becomes a very tense affair if there is not also unity in truth.

3. He wanted to restore their confidence in the gospel

This leads us on to the apostle's third concern — namely that the Christians among the three towns should attain **'all**

riches of the full assurance of understanding, to the knowledge of the mystery of God, both of the Father and of Christ' (2:2). Essentially Paul wanted his readers to regain complete confidence in the gospel because this had been shaken by the emphases of the new arrivals. Here Paul uses the word **'mystery'** as he did in 1:26-27. 'Mystery' is a word that occurs frequently in the apostle's vocabulary. In everyday English, a mystery is something that we have to work out, an enigma, puzzle or secret. Someone with a supple and agile mind might just be able to crack the riddle. We can, if we are not careful, read that meaning back into the Bible. When Paul says in Ephesians 5:32 that the fact that a good relationship between a husband and his wife mirrors in a small way the bond that exists between Christ and his church is a 'great mystery', we suspect that he means that it is next to impossible to understand it. By 'mystery' however, the apostle meant something that was once hidden and that we would not have known unless God had seen fit to reveal it. It was once a closed book; now it is an open secret. In the fullest sense, this 'mystery' is the gospel, God's way of salvation revealed in Jesus Christ. Since we would never have understood what salvation entailed without the coming of God's Son, it is in fact, 'the mystery of Christ' (Eph. 3:4). In him God has revealed what we could never have discovered. The grand focus of this revelation is Christ himself. He is the mystery that God has revealed to a largely uncomprehending world.

At this point, we need to note Paul's words in verse 3. In Christ **'are hidden all the treasures of wisdom and knowledge'**. This is aimed at the new teachers who urged that they could provide access to new and greater blessings over and above the blessings that mere conversion, and therefore union with Christ, could guarantee. But if 'all the treasures' are available to every believer in Christ as such, then there are no more blessings to be had beyond those that are available in him. Those who listened to the new teachers would eventually find that their enjoyment and appreciation of Christ were subtly diminished, on the understanding that the true spiritual elite needed more than he could provide. Paul, by contrast, wanted his readers to be amazed at the greatness of Christ. His use of the word **'wisdom'**, for instance, touches on the way that our Saviour has achieved the impossible. The justice of God demands the death of every sinner. The love of God yearns for the salvation of sinners. In Christ, the wisdom of God has found a way to satisfy the claims of love and justice. The only fitting response to such a wonderful Saviour is praise. The newcomers in Colosse, however, by suggesting that Christ alone is not sufficient to guarantee the fulness of blessing, had found a subtle way not to praise Jesus, but to belittle him and undermine his people.

Paul's fear for his readers (2:4)

Some commentators argue that Paul had his sights on a particular person in verse 4. This seems unlikely because he was not frightened to name names when this was necessary and no one person is singled out for mention here. It seems rather that Paul was concerned about a particular style, or approach, that had become the hallmark of the new teachers. It was not so much their arguments that troubled Paul as their presentational skills. Of course there is nothing inherently wrong in being persuasive. Paul himself could be a very effective advocate for the gospel (2 Cor. 5:11). The problem is that the believers in Colosse had been confronted by a group of men who had proved very adept at making a potentially dangerous brand of teaching seem attractive.

In recent times we have seen the rise of the 'spin doctor', the expert whose task is to make sure that his political masters always come up smelling of roses, whatever the twists and turns of events. There is now, however, an increasingly uneasy feeling that the world of politics has become a triumph of style over substance. The merits of a politician's case are no longer what counts. The critical thing is that the politician himself should project a good image. He should look his best, charm the voters and come over as someone who is likeable and trustworthy. This is a disturbing trend in politics because it assumes that the voters are too shallow to see beyond mere presentation.

Back in the first century, Paul sensed the rise of a similar breed that had won the approval of believers and churches because they came across well. Their arguments were not particularly effective, but they got under the guard of believers because they themselves seemed plausible. They are still with us. In some parts of the evangelical scene the leaders who attract attention are more notable for their star quality than their capacity for exegesis, more celebrated for the force of personality than the force of truth. Paul's own pursuit of scrupulous integrity in communicating the gospel is refreshing: 'We have renounced the hidden things of shame, not walking in craftiness nor handling the word of God deceitfully, but by manifestation of the truth commending ourselves to every man's conscience in the sight of God' (2 Cor. 4:2). At the end of the day, a question needs to be faced. What drew people to align themselves with a particular teacher? Was it the drawing power of the Christ that he held up before them, or a pleasant manner and a well-honed technique?

Paul's delight in his readers (2:5)

Verse 5 begins with a pair of contrasting statements: '**... though I am absent in the flesh, yet I am with you in spirit.**' In the first statement, Paul addresses the fact that he was a stranger to most of his readers in Colosse. Under house arrest in Rome, he was several hundred miles away. Some might have raised the objection that the ongoing tussle for the identity of the three churches was none of his business. He was an outsider and a stranger. In his second statement, the apostle sought to waylay this concern. By saying that he was with the Colossian believers **'in spirit'**, the apostle meant them to understand that he identified with them very strongly indeed. He felt at one with them in their longings, aspirations and concerns.

It is interesting to note that he used much the same language when writing to the church at Corinth (1 Cor. 5:3-5). On that occasion, he was 'absent in body' because he was in Ephesus, but his concern for a church facing a difficult case of discipline was so complete that he had been able to form an accurate opinion of the rights and wrongs of the matter as though he had been there to hear the evidence. Modern Christians can experience something similar. The gospel can create an immediate bond with people that we don't know and have never met — for example, when we pray for believers who are undergoing persecution in other parts of the world. Even though we have not been introduced to them, they are our family.

It is also worth noting that, although Paul was troubled by the situation among the three churches, he had also heard things, presumably from Epaphras, which encouraged him greatly. At this point the apostle commended the believers using two military terms. The first, translated **'good order'**, describes the way that soldiers on the battlefield would close ranks to prevent enemy penetration. During the Napoleonic wars, one of the duties of British sergeants was to repeat the command, 'Close up!' Even as some fell to enemy gunfire and the ranks were thinned, it was vital to close up. Gaps can be exploited. It seems that the believers in Colosse were good at holding one another up. Desertions were few. Generally speaking, nerve held because each one buoyed up the spirits of his neighbour and when the honourably wounded had to quit the fray, others would step into the ranks.

Paul also commended their **'steadfastness'**. Their **'faith in Christ'** was not flimsy. It had a dogged quality to it. This augured well for the future. The church in Colosse faced a genuine threat, but it had already learned the knack of closing ranks in a stout, enduring fashion. And although he was not physically present, Paul stood in the ranks alongside his fellow soldiers. Would he see the same qualities in us? And are we as ready as he was to see where the ranks are being thinned by enemy action and to step boldly into the breach?

Conclusion

One thing that emerges clearly as we read these verses is Paul's readiness to identify himself closely with the interests of a group of Christians that he had not met in person. He was elated at their encouragements and deeply concerned by the challenges that confronted them. It reminds us of his words to another group of believers, where he spoke of 'what comes upon me daily: my deep concern for all the churches. Who is weak, and I am not weak? Who is made to stumble, and I do not burn with indignation?' (2 Cor. 11:28-29). Faced with his example, we would do well to ask ourselves whether we are on the way to becoming 'world Christians', who have a thoughtful, well-informed concern for our brothers and sisters in a variety of situations throughout the world. While there is always the danger of 'information overload' and we must recognize that no one person can take an interest in the work of God in every single place, most Christians in the developed world could do with broadening their sympathies and widening the scope of their prayers.

7.
True spiritual progress

Please read Colossians 2:6-7

Paul wrote this letter to a church that was in danger of being captured. There was a real possibility that the church in Colosse might be taken over from within and weaned away from the original principles on which it had been founded. Paul was concerned by this development. If people accepted the agenda of the new teachers, there was a real danger that they would end up thinking less of Christ. After all, if spiritual excellence involves embracing something new and different in addition to Christ, if the truly blessed life calls for faith in Christ and more besides, this can only mean that Christ by himself is not sufficient.

At this point we need to be aware of a corresponding danger. If, as Paul did, we resist the claims of those who suggest that moving on in the Christian life means moving beyond mere faith in Christ, we must be equally clear that there is a place for Christian progress. Paul did not want the believers in Colosse to stagnate. The stagnant Christian is a disgrace. The New Testament insists that believers must seek to advance in their Christian development: 'As newborn babes, desire the pure milk of the word, that you may grow thereby' (1 Peter 2:2). Spiritual babies should grow. Such growth is natural and normal: 'Abide in me, and I in you. As the branch cannot bear fruit of itself, unless it abides in the vine, neither can you, unless you abide in me. I am the vine, you are the branches. He who abides in me, and I in him, bears much fruit; for without me you can do nothing' (John 15:4-5). The branches of Christ's vine should bear fruit. There is something wrong with branches that remain bare.

In all fairness, we should observe that some Christians who accept mistaken views of holiness do so out of a genuine longing to be holy. I have known people who have been enticed by sinless perfectionism or the old 'higher life' teaching who were mainly attracted to these ideas because they wanted to be the best that a saved sinner could be out of gratitude for Jesus. This leaves us facing a question of the utmost importance. Given that Christian progress is an urgent necessity for every true believer, what form does growth in grace actually take? Having come to faith in Christ, do we grow in Christ, or does spiritual growth somehow take us beyond Christ? This is the subject that Paul addresses in verses 6-7.

'As you have received Christ ... so walk in him' (2:6)

Paul's starting point is that every Christian has **'received Christ'**. The same phrase is often used today. We hear of evangelistic meetings where so many people 'received Christ'. We can only hope that all who use this phrase mean the same as Paul meant. In saying that they had 'received Christ', the apostle meant that a number of things were true of his readers in Colosse.

1. Their faith was founded on historical fact

In the first place, they had made a wholehearted endorsement of the central facts of Christ's life and ministry: 'Moreover, brethren, I declare to you the gospel which I preached to you, which also you received and in which you stand, by which also you are saved, if you hold fast that word which I preached to you — unless you believed in vain. For I delivered to you first of all that which I also received: that Christ died for our sins according to the Scriptures, and that he was buried, and that he rose again the third day according to the Scriptures' (1 Cor. 15:1-4). Faith is based on facts. If the events of Jesus' life revealed in the Gospels are not true, if he was not born of a virgin, if he did not go around doing good and preaching the way of salvation, if his death and resurrection never happened, we are under no compulsion to commit ourselves to him. Why entrust yourself to someone if the only account of his life and work is untrustworthy?

2. They were united to Christ by faith

Faith as Paul understood it, however, involves more than a hearty agreement that what the Bible says about Jesus really happened. Faith involves entrusting all that I am to the Jesus who is revealed in the Bible. Faith unites me to Christ. It makes me one with him. Believers become so completely linked with Christ that the Bible speaks of their being 'in Christ'. Their destiny and their future are bound up with his. Have you received Christ in that sense? Do you agree with the facts concerning him? Have you surrendered your life to his control and welcomed him into the very core of your being?

3. They acknowledged Christ as their Lord

It is noticeable that the Christ whom we receive is **'the Lord'**. All Christians receive 'the Lord'. Nothing else is possible. That is who Jesus is. Even so, there are teachers who say that the Christian life takes place in two stages: at the outset, we receive Christ as Saviour; further down the road, some, but not all, believers receive him as Lord. Teaching of this kind is a terrible distortion of the gospel. Growth in grace ceases to be a binding obligation for all believers and becomes an optional extra for an elite handful. Isaac Watts' words, 'Love so amazing, so divine, demands my soul, my life, my all', lose all their force. A godly life is no longer the least that a grateful heart can bring to Christ; it is merely a laudable aspiration for those who feel drawn to it because they like that sort of thing, those who, by temperament, are natural enthusiasts.

This teaching also presents us with a very different Jesus from the one in the Bible. Jesus saves because he is Lord. Salvation is much too great a task for a mere superhero. Rescuing people from sin, death and hell is beyond any run-of-the-mill prophet. Only the sovereign Ruler of heaven and earth can save sinners. The gospel is not only an appeal to sinners, but the assertion of a king's right to rule. When Jesus said to his first disciples, 'Follow me', he expected them to comply. They were so much in awe of his authority that they did so. In coming to Christ, we come to one who makes demands on us. He made us and bought us and has a right to lay his yoke on our shoulders.

This is what lies behind Paul's phrase: **'... so walk in him.'** If we have received Christ, there is an ethical imperative. We must make a disciplined and systematic attempt to bring the whole of life into line with his commandments. We see the same compelling logic in 2 Peter 1:5-8: '... for this very reason, giving all diligence, add to your faith virtue, to virtue knowledge, to knowledge self-control, to self-control perseverance, to perseverance godliness, to godliness brotherly kindness, and to brotherly kindness love. For if these things are yours and abound, you will be neither barren nor unfruitful in the knowledge of our Lord Jesus Christ.'

Progress, then, is not an option for the favoured few, but the will of Christ for all his people. Nevertheless, having received Christ, we do not walk in new and uncharted directions. We walk in the way of the Christ whom we have received.

Rooted in Christ and built up in Christ (2:7)

There is no doubt that Paul wanted his readers to make spiritual excellence a priority. In the early part of verse 7 he uses colourful imagery, which, in effect, poses a question: 'Given that the roots are secure, does any growth appear above ground?' At first sight, it might seem that Paul's imagery is a little confused, speaking of roots to begin with, and then of the growth of a building. Roots below ground normally lead to a trunk and branches. In secular Greek, however, it was not unusual to refer to the foundations of a building as its roots. At any rate, the main thrust of his argument is clear. Having made a good beginning, the Christian must not give way to complacency and stop there.

We see the same logic at work in 1 Corinthians 3:11-15, where Paul writes that 'No other foundation can anyone lay than that which is laid, which is Jesus Christ. Now if anyone builds on this foundation with gold, silver, precious stones, wood, hay, straw, each one's work will become clear; for the Day will declare it, because it will be revealed by fire; and the fire will test each one's work, of what sort it is. If anyone's work which he has built on it endures, he will receive a reward. If anyone's work is burned, he will suffer loss; but he himself will be saved, yet so as through fire' (1 Cor. 3:11-15). All Christians have one glorious fact in common. Each and every one of them has a solid foundation that will stand the most searching test of all. Build on Christ, and you will outlast the world itself. When the heavens and the earth are shaken by the great and terrible Day of Judgement, you will be secure. Not all believers, however, build on that foundation in the same way. Some use shoddy and perishable materials; others the choicest and most precious assets they can bring. The quality of the foundation surely deserves the best superstructure that we can erect: 'Therefore, leaving the discussion of the elementary principles of Christ, let us go on to perfection, not laying again the foundation of repentance from dead works and of faith toward God' (Heb. 6:1).

Progress, however, though it is a moral and spiritual imperative, is always 'in Christ'. Those who are rooted in Christ are not built up by moving away from Christ to something else, whether that something else be the sacraments, certain spiritual disciplines, or even various experiences of the Holy Spirit. Christ is not only the roots, but also the trunk and branches of a successful Christian life; he is both the foundation and the building. We begin in him and we grow in him.

Be established in faith (2:7)

Again Paul strikes a vigorous blow against the idea that it is ever acceptable for the Christian to be static. The believers in Colosse had been taught to entrust themselves to Jesus Christ; now they must entrust themselves to him all the more.

At this point, Paul's phrase, **'the faith'**, does not so much mean the body of doctrine that Christians believe as 'the faith' that they had been encouraged to put in Christ. It began when they first learned to trust him; now it must grow and develop. At the same time, it is not entirely possible to separate teaching people to believe in Jesus from teaching them the truth about Jesus; they cannot become Christians at all without a minimum of vital information. Men and women need to be told the truth about the fact that God made them and that they are accountable to him. They need to know about their guilt before God and enough about Jesus' life, death and resurrection to grasp the fact that he is everything that they could possibly need in a Saviour.

But, while a basic minimum of information may be enough to bring a person to faith in Christ, it will not be enough to bring him or her to maturity. Paul made the same point elsewhere in his writings: '... we should no longer be children, tossed to and fro and carried about with every wind of doctrine, by the trickery of men, in the cunning craftiness of deceitful plotting, but, speaking the truth in love, may grow up in all things into him who is the head — Christ' (Eph. 4:14-15). It is worth noting that Paul's emphasis here is in keeping with the point he is making in Colossians 2:6-7. Growing up in spiritual things does not mean moving past the Christ who saved us and leaving him behind, but growing up into Christ: 'Brethren, do not be children in understanding; however, in malice be babes, but in understanding be mature' (1 Cor. 14:20).

This is a sharp challenge to much of modern evangelicalism, which thrives on a cult of the infantile and the asinine. A thirst to know more about Jesus is rare enough to be refreshing. Few things are more stimulating than a hunger to understand more of God and his ways. It is wonderfully heartening when we encounter someone who has an insatiable appetite for sermons and good Christian literature. Paul's emphasis here is both wholesome and sane. There is no doubt that a certain kind of preoccupation with doctrine can make us arid and unappealing. We become obsessed with the minutiae of theological discourse. Paul's concern, by contrast, is not that we should become established in truth for its own sake, but established in truth about Christ so that we might trust and appreciate him all the more. A person who is obsessed with Jesus cannot help but begin to resemble him. People like that are attractive. At the outset of our Christian lives we were taught things about Jesus that drew us to him. The more we learned, the more our love was kindled. It follows that the more the doctrine that we learn is about Christ, whether directly or indirectly, the more we shall depend upon him and indeed, become like him: 'But we all, with unveiled face, beholding as in a mirror the glory of the Lord, are being transformed into the same image from glory to glory, just as by the Spirit of the Lord' (2 Cor. 3:18).

Be thankful (2:7)

Paul concludes his list of exhortations by noting that believers are to abound in our faith **'with thanksgiving'**. Christianity at its best will always be backward-looking. I don't mean by this that it will be nostalgic and reluctant to face the demands of serving Christ in today's world — though some Christians are certainly like that — but rather that it will return again and again to Calvary out of sheer amazement for all that Jesus did for his people. It is a bad sign if we lose our sense of being stunned at the wonder of grace. A thankful heart understands grace, but when our thanks dry up, it is because we have begun to think that heaven is no more than our due. The man who gets what he deserves has no one to thank but himself, but the man who is given far more than he could ever deserve, and who has been treated with lavish but completely unmerited kindness, should surely be grateful. Thankfulness points away from ourselves and from what we have done, and enjoys with amazement all that Christ has done: 'For you know the grace of our Lord Jesus Christ, that though he was rich, yet for your sakes he became poor, that you through his poverty might become rich' (2 Cor. 8:9).

Conclusion

Paul was ambitious for the believers in first-century Colosse. He wanted them to yearn for spiritual excellence with a deep longing. He pressed this upon them, arguing that a good beginning by itself is not enough. His logic is simple but compelling. A good start to the Christian life calls for on-going progress. For those who have received Christ, continuing to walk in him is not merely desirable: it is essential. What use is a foundation without a superstructure? In the same way, while the Christian life begins when we first entrust ourselves to Jesus Christ, faith does not stop at that point. We begin by faith in God's Son and we continue as that faith grows and develops.

Furthermore, Paul was convinced that simple gratitude for all that Christ had done for them left those first-century Christians with no alternative. How far do we share this longing for ourselves? If we do, we need to ensure that our desire for spiritual progress never becomes detached from devotion to Jesus. True spiritual life begins in Christ, continues in Christ and will find its grand climax in Christ: 'For of him and through him and to him are all things, to whom be glory for ever. Amen' (Rom. 11:36).

8.
Don't let yourself be kidnapped!

Please read Colossians 2:8-10

Christians often have a wry smile when they read what the apostle Peter had to say about the apostle Paul: 'Our beloved brother Paul, according to the wisdom given to him, has written to you, as also in all his epistles, speaking in them of these things, in which are some things hard to understand, which untaught and unstable people twist to their own destruction, as they do also the rest of the Scriptures' (2 Peter 3:15-16). Do you ever find some of Paul's writings 'hard to understand'? The section in Colossians 2 from verse 8 to verse 15 certainly makes for a demanding read. This is partly because it is a miracle of condensation. The apostle said many weighty things in a few words. This means that the reader, and for that matter the preacher, is faced with a dual task. On the one hand, it is important that we retain a grip on the main thrust of Paul's argument. We cannot afford to lose sight of the general direction of the letter as a whole. On the other hand, we must strive to give each individual statement due attention. Move too quickly from point to point, and we may miss something precious on the way.

This section is also important for another reason. The church in Colosse had been infiltrated by new teachers, unscrupulous interlopers with an agenda very different from

Paul's. Ever since that time, scholars have been at pains to establish just what these newcomers actually taught. Here, in verses 8-15, Paul gives us more of an idea about what his rivals were saying than in any other part of the letter.

We begin our examination of this section by noting that verses 8-10 contain a warning. Some modern Christians are uneasy about the appropriateness of a ministry of warning. It can seem negative, even unloving. Warning, however, was an authentic note of Paul's teaching. When he left Ephesus he urged his friends there: 'Remember that for three years I did not cease to warn everyone night and day with tears' (Acts 20:31). He feared that 'After my departure savage wolves will come in among you, not sparing the flock. Also from among yourselves men will rise up, speaking perverse things, to draw away the disciples after themselves' (Acts 20:29-30). What kind of love is it that fails to alert dear friends to serious danger?

Don't let yourself be kidnapped (2:8)

In September 2003, British newspapers were full of the story of Matthew Scot, a young man who had chosen to take a 'gap year' before commencing his studies at Oxford University. He was one of a group of tourists on a trekking holiday in Colombia who were seized by terrorists wanting wealthy Western hostages to ransom in order to fund their drug-running operations. Matthew, a resourceful young man, threw himself down a ravine and then walked through dense jungle until some tribal people led him to safety. He is back in Britain now. Paul feared the dangers of a spiritual 'smash-and-grab raid' that would see the believers in Colosse taken as hostages.

The word **'cheat'** is not the best translation of a Greek word that only occurs once in the New Testament. It actually means 'take captive'. It describes what happens when victorious soldiers seize booty from their defeated enemies, or even take their prisoners away as slaves. Paul urged the believers to beware in case they unwittingly became the prey of those who had brought the new teaching.

Paul makes the assumption here that those who do not teach the authentic gospel are essentially spiritual predators. What this meant in Colosse was that the newcomers, while presenting their message as the way to spiritual liberty, would actually deprive believers of their freedom in Christ by enslaving them to a set of principles that were only superficially Christian. The same process can still be observed today. Christians can be led away from the simplicity of the gospel by unscrupulous teachers who pass their message off as the real thing by cloaking it with Christian terminology. Use the right kind of words, and you can feed people a cocktail of half-truths mixed with falsehoods, which is sub-Christian, or even anti-Christian. Some believers are gullible. The Christian who can be led by the nose has no defence against such spiritual predators. The antidote is discernment. Sadly, this gift is not valued as much as it once was. It is best fostered in churches with a strong commitment to teaching. On the other hand, you can almost guarantee that churches that place a low premium on teaching God's Word will turn out believers who are naïve: 'We should no longer be children, tossed to and fro and carried about with every wind of doctrine, by the trickery of men, in the cunning craftiness of deceitful plotting' (Eph. 4:14).

Every Christian has a responsibility to develop a mature grasp of the essentials of the Christian faith. This is our only defence against teachers who pervert the Christian message. What steps are we taking to make sure that we progress beyond an ill-formed and immature grasp of Christian teaching?

Know your enemy (2:8)

Paul was concerned that the believers in Colosse might be taken captive. He feared that they might be won over to the side of something that he termed **'philosophy and empty deceit'**. By **'philosophy'** he did not mean an academic subject that could be studied at university. The word is also sometimes used to refer to a 'world view', a set of convictions about the meaning of life. The first-century Jewish historian Josephus used it in that way when he said that the Jews in his day had three philosophies. He meant the teachings of the Pharisees, the Sadducees and the Essenes. Seen from that angle, Christianity is a philosophy. In that sense, a philosophy or world view is a set of beliefs about God, the universe and our place in it as human beings. At the same time, Christians would insist that theirs is the only true philosophy, given that Jesus said, 'I am the way, the truth, and the life. No one comes to the Father except through me' (John 14:6).

Understood in this way, there is a sense in which everyone has a philosophy. No one is completely without opinions on what *The Hitchhiker's Guide to the Galaxy* called the question of 'life, the universe and everything'. Some have thought through their opinions with care; others have amassed a set of half-baked prejudices. Surely we owe it to ourselves to give this matter serious thought! If the fate of our souls is at stake, there is nothing to be said for being slipshod. It is not as if any philosophy or world view will do. In many areas of life a mistaken conclusion will only have trivial consequences, but when it comes to the issues of time and eternity, heaven and hell, we simply cannot afford to pin our all on a mistaken set of conclusions.

At this point, however, Paul used the word 'philosophy' in a purely negative sense. He coupled it with the phrase **'empty deceit'**. Theirs was a man-made system. They were advocating something that was not only untrue, but also hollow, incorrect and devoid of substance. It made great claims, but there was nothing in it.

Can we put a name to it? Scholars have tried over the years to identify what is called the 'Colossian heresy'. Later in the passage Paul gives some hints as to its true nature. It seems to have been a pick-and-mix fusion of Judaism and an early form of what came to be called Gnosticism. Here in verse 8 Paul makes a number of preliminary observations that are equally true of many brands of false teaching.

1. Their teaching was of human origin

First of all, what the newcomers taught was **'according to the tradition of men'**. **'Tradition'** is a word that sometimes makes evangelical Christians nervous. They are all too conscious that the Roman Catholic Church teaches that its traditions have the same weight as Scripture. There is, however, a proper tradition that Bible-loving Christians should appreciate and respect. Paul described it to Timothy in this way: 'The things that you have heard from me among many witnesses, commit these to faithful men who will be able to teach others also' (2 Tim. 2:2). Passing on what Jesus taught clearly and faithfully from one generation to the next is tradition at its best.

Unfortunately something quite different was taking place in Colosse. Paul detected fertile human imaginations at work. Far from transmitting the message of Jesus without embellishment or adulteration, the new teachers had distorted the gospel by inventing elements of their own. When it comes to doctrine — that is to say, 'what is taught' — responsible Christian communicators must be rigid and unbending conservatives. We have no right to innovate. There is a fixed body of truth to propagate and defend. We are to 'contend earnestly for the faith which was once for all delivered to the saints' (Jude 1:3).

2. They had an unhealthy obsession with the hidden forces of the spiritual world

Paul noted, secondly, that the world view or 'philosophy' of the men who were troubling the church in Colosse was **'according to the basic principles of the world'**. At this point we have to note a difference of opinion among Bible-believing scholars as to how this statement should be trans-lated. If the NKJV rendering quoted above is correct, Paul was essentially saying that the teaching of the newcomers was rudimentary. They tried to portray their message as something refined, as advanced teaching for the mature spiritual sophisticate. According to this reading of the text, Paul's response was dismissive. For all the exaggerated claims made for it, it was really all very elementary!

There is good reason, however, to adopt a different reading — namely, that the teaching of these men was according to the 'elemental spirits'. This fits in with Paul's insistence in verse 10 that Christ has authority over 'all principality and power' and his caution in verse 18 against undue preoccupation with angels. It would seem that the new teachers were concerned with the hidden forces that operate in the spiritual world. It is undoubtedly true that there are powers at work that we cannot see. Even today many reli-gions start with the assumption that because these entities can help us or harm us we need to learn how to enlist their aid or how to get them off our backs. The Colossian teachers were putting themselves forward as experts in this area. They could persuade the benign powers, the angels, to come to the aid of their clients and they could teach ways of warding off the evil machinations of the dark powers. Even today, evangelical Christians are not completely immune to this kind of thinking. In some circles there is a fixation with knowing how to deal with both angels and demons as the need arises.

3. Christ is the only true teacher

Paul's point was simply that this kind of preoccupation is unhealthy. Both that and the fascination with traditions concocted by mere men are **'not according to Christ'**. Ultimately, he is the only true teacher. Other teachers only deserve our attention insofar as they accurately reflect what he has said. Since he is 'the head of all principality and power' (2:10), he is greater than all the unseen powers put together.

Know your friend (2:9-10)

The new teachers hinted that mere faith in Christ was not enough. They could never have thought that for a moment if they had appreciated just how wonderful Jesus is. Paul's phrase, **'In him dwells all the fulness of the Godhead bodily'** (2:9), was intended to remind his readers that Jesus is wonderful beyond description. When we describe him we are frustrated by the limitations of language. Superlative words like 'wonderful', 'superb', 'sublime', 'magnificent' and 'glorious' let us down. His greatness goes far beyond all human ability to describe it. Paul's response to the newcomers is both simple and devastating. By suggesting that the believers in Colosse needed something in addition to Christ alone, they were being dismissive about the greatest person in the entire universe.

'All the fulness of the Godhead' is a very big phrase. In talking about **'fulness'** Paul was borrowing one of the newcomers' own pet phrases. Here he applies it to the

Creator of the universe, the Lord of angels, the Judge of mankind, the one who takes moral failure with such holy seriousness that he drowned the world in a great flood, the one who inspired prophets and apostles, and so gave the world the miracle on paper known as the Bible. That God is present in human form in the man named Jesus. And when we consider Jesus, it is not as though God is merely present to some extent. Nothing of God is missing. The Almighty is present in Christ in all his attributes. The all-seeing, all-knowing God dwells in Christ. The God of perfect holiness and awesome power, of towering wrath and tender yet majestic grace, has come to mankind in a human body and wearing a human face.

And because 'all the fulness of the Godhead' is there in Christ, there is no more of God to be known than can be found in him. You will not discover more of God by moving on from Christ. Leave him behind, and you leave God behind. No fulness can exceed this. This is why Paul could tell the believers in Colosse, **'You are complete in him'** (2:10). If you have Jesus, there is nothing more to be had. The new teachers then and their modern counterparts now argue that we are not complete until we have moved past mere initiation, but Jesus is so supremely glorious that it is an insult to his glory and greatness to suggest that we need more. Is he, of all people, being what he is, not enough to satisfy the longings of every human heart?

Conclusion

This passage alerts us to the danger, on the one hand, of falling prey to religious charlatans who argue that spiritual fulness is only to be found if we add new insights or experiences to the simplicity that is to be found in Jesus Christ. On the other hand, it is also clear that the best way to avoid being taken in is to cultivate large views of the Son of God, to ensure that he fills our mental and spiritual horizon, that our hearts are full of Christ. No greater blessing exists than to know the love of Jesus. To be in Christ is as good as it gets.

In that case, how high is our estimate of Christ? God thinks everything of him. He sees his own glory and perfections completely and fully reflected in the face of Jesus Christ. The man who owned a whole galaxy but did not have Christ might as well be a pauper, while the person who has Jesus and nothing else at all in this life has staggering wealth because he has 'all the fulness of Godhead'. Without Jesus, nothing that you have is worth anything. With Jesus, he, and he alone, is more precious than mountains of gold and jewels, than all the myriads of stars and planets in the Milky Way.

In the end, everything revolves around this one great issue. You may have many needs, but no need is greater than your need of Christ and, until you have made him your own by faith, there will always be a colossal piece of unfinished business waiting to be resolved. Don't delay until you can say with the apostle John, 'And of his fulness we have all received, and grace for grace' (John 1:16).

9.
Don't belittle conversion!

Please read Colossians 2:11-15

In the autumn of 2003 the Safeway supermarket chain, one of the largest in the UK, was bought by one of its rivals, Morrisons. It transpired that there had also been a bid from the largest competitor in the supermarket world, ASDA. If this had succeeded, ASDA's American parent company, Wal-Mart, would have gained a disproportionate share of the British market. Of course there is nothing new about a take-over bid in the world of commerce. Indeed, local churches can also fall prey to a takeover bid. By that, I don't mean that small churches are gobbled up by larger ones, as happens in the world of business. I mean rather that a group of people can gain control of a church and, in doing so, capture it for a very different set of principles and a different ethos from those that it held at the outset. It sometimes happens when a church calls a new minister without being aware of his real agenda.

The apostle feared that something of this sort was happening in Colosse. Plausible men with strong personalities were steering the church away from its original beliefs with the enticing suggestion that they had something better to offer than the gospel taught by Epaphras, the church's founder. They could offer the gospel plus some added extra. This is

why Paul warned the believers in Colosse not to let themselves be taken captive (2:8), recruited for an agenda that
was less than truly Christian. He then went on to make the
point that the person who has Christ is complete, since the
whole of God's fulness is found in Jesus (2:9-10).

Now Paul goes on to make much more of the same theme.
Jesus Christ is inexpressibly wonderful. He has no rivals or
equals. He is both the most remarkable man who ever lived
and God to the utmost degree. It follows that to become a
Christian, to be united by faith to this glorious Saviour, is an
extraordinary privilege. We cannot overstate the importance
of conversion. The newcomers trying to seize control of the
church in Colosse argued that something even greater lay
beyond conversion. Paul's response in these verses is to
describe conversion in such glowing terms that the very idea
that there is something better to follow is shown up for the
hollow nonsense that it is.

At conversion, believers were circumcised (2:11)

The fact that Paul chose to speak in these terms suggests that
those who were out to capture the church at Colosse insisted
that their followers should be circumcised. Some readers of
this letter will know that there was a similar emphasis among
the churches in Galatia. Christians who had not been circumcised were coming under pressure to have the operation. The
two situations, however, were actually quite different. In
Galatia church members from non-Jewish backgrounds were
urged to undergo circumcision on the grounds that it was
necessary for salvation, a view that Paul denounced as 'a
different gospel' (Gal. 1:6). In Colosse it seems that circumcision was being pressed on people as a means of **'putting
off the body of the sins of the flesh'** (2:11). Those who
advocated it saw it as a ritual of consecration. The very fact

that it was a painful procedure indicated that it was only for those who meant business. (Again and again we meet in Colossians the idea that the newcomers appealed to that side of human nature that likes to belong to the 'in crowd', the initiated. You could enjoy the camaraderie that went with being one of a select band.) As baptism became the rite of initiation for all believers, circumcision was a second rite of initiation for the elite handful who were serious about making a decisive break with sin. Submit to circumcision in this way, and you could congratulate yourself that you were no dabbler. It is not difficult to imagine the openings this gave for smug self-satisfaction, on the one hand, nor how those outside the charmed circle would have resented the patronizing outlook of the insiders, on the other.

Paul's answer is that all this emphasis on circumcision was unnecessary. It was pointless, redundant. This is because there is a real sense in which every Christian, whether Jewish or otherwise, has been circumcised already. By this the apostle did not mean the medical procedure, but a different kind of circumcision altogether, one that was **'made without hands'**. It was, in short, a spiritual circumcision. When the Holy Spirit makes new persons of us there is a sense in which we bear the mark of Christ, but this is not the kind of physical mark that Jewish men still bear in their bodies.

Indeed, actual physical circumcision, as it was practised in Old Testament days, was only ever meant to be an outward symbol of this greater circumcision. One of the blessings promised in Deuteronomy if the people of Israel returned to God after a period of backsliding was that 'The LORD your God will circumcise your heart and the heart of your descendants, to love the LORD your God with all your heart and with all your soul, that you may live' (Deut. 30:6).

In Romans 2 Paul made the point that this inward circumcision is vastly more important than a minor surgical procedure that only makes a mark on the outside of a man: 'For he is not a Jew who is one outwardly, nor is circumcision that which is outward in the flesh; but he is a Jew who is one inwardly; and circumcision is that of the heart, in the Spirit, not in the letter; whose praise is not from men but from God' (Rom. 2:28-29).

In Colosse, the new teachers argued that physical circumcision was the proof of a man's willingness to live the victorious life, a life of consistent victory over sin. Every now and then a new form of this same emphasis breaks out and believers are encouraged to think that sin can be dealt with in one dramatic crisis. Those who embrace this kind of thinking fail to appreciate just how virulent and durable sin can be. Paul wanted his readers to understand that spiritual circumcision produces a clean break with sin of a different kind. Conversion does not mean that sin is gone for good in this life, but it does mean the end of sin as the dominant power in our hearts and minds.

Have you been circumcised? The medical procedure is neither here nor there: 'For in Christ Jesus neither circumcision nor uncircumcision avails anything, but faith working through love' (Gal. 5:6). But has Christ transformed you from within and set his mark on your soul? If so, while sin may not have been completely eradicated, it will no longer have the grip it once did on your affections, your pleasures and your habits of thought.

At conversion, believers were baptized (2:12-13)

Just as the circumcision mentioned in verse 11 was not an operation with a knife, so too, the baptism mentioned in verses 12-13 is not a ritual involving water. If physical circumcision portrays the circumcision of the heart, baptism in water is an outward symbol of a different and more important baptism altogether. A person may never be baptized in water, yet go to heaven. This other baptism is essential for any prospect of a happy and secure eternity. At the same time, baptism in water is certainly a vivid illustration of the inward change of heart, mind and direction that make up conversion to Christ. The rite of baptism takes the form of a burial, not in earth but water, and a re-emergence. These correspond to what Paul describes in these verses as a death and resurrection.

Language like this tells us that conversion is a dramatic change. It is far more than a change of opinions, or even a change of lifestyle. It goes far deeper than the most radical overhaul of the personality known to psychiatry. When someone becomes a Christian he or she doesn't merely acquire a new set of convictions, or begin to act with greater moral consistency. Paul's description of the change is breathtaking. The person the Christian once was has ceased to exist. A believer is a new person altogether. What happens to the new Christian is intimately and powerfully linked with the death and resurrection of Jesus. United to Christ by faith, the believer is both **'buried with him'** and **'raised with him'** (2:12).

What does this mean in practice? Before we became Christians we were in a bad way. Paul describes his readers as having been **'dead in ... trespasses'** (2:13), spiritually and morally lifeless and incapable of responding to God. They were also uncircumcised. This may well mean that they had not yet experienced the spiritual circumcision mentioned in verse 11. I tend to think, however, that in this case, Paul was using the word in the same way that King David referred to the Philistines as 'the uncircumcised'. Those who are not yet Christians don't belong to the people of God. Every converted person was once like that. But that person has ceased to exist. He is quite dead and a new person has taken his place.

Paul used the same logic in Romans 6:3-10: 'Do you not know that as many of us as were baptized into Christ Jesus were baptized into his death? Therefore we were buried with him through baptism into death, that just as Christ was raised from the dead by the glory of the Father, even so we also should walk in newness of life. For if we have been united together in the likeness of his death, certainly we also shall be in the likeness of his resurrection, knowing this, that our old man was crucified with him, that the body of sin might be done away with, that we should no longer be slaves of sin. For he who has died has been freed from sin. Now if we died with Christ, we believe that we shall also live with him, knowing that Christ, having been raised from the dead, dies no more. Death no longer has dominion over him. For the death that he died, he died to sin once for all; but the life that he lives, he lives to God.'

This should thrill every Christian to the core. As believers, we have not merely been renovated, or brushed up. We are new people with a radically new kind of life within. Until Jesus comes again and makes all things new, biological death still awaits us and sin is a malign force that needs to be subdued each day, but none of this detracts from the glory of it. Conversion to Christ does not merely involve some cosmetic and superficial changes. It is a spiritual baptism in which we undergo a real death and a dramatic resurrection, having become brand new persons altogether.

At conversion, believers were forgiven (2:13-15)

The subject of forgiveness is introduced in the second part of verse 13. This is not partial or conditional forgiveness. God does not forgive us only up to a point, or insist that we pass certain tests first before we are deemed worthy of his pardon. (If we had to clean up our act first, the task would be hopeless.) Paul writes of total forgiveness, the forgiveness of **'all trespasses'**. Nothing is more necessary than this. We desperately need it. And nothing is more exciting and exhilarating on this side of heaven. There is no experience to match the free-grace experience, the joy that comes from knowing that everything about us that once offended God has been wiped clean away. Paul describes God's forgiveness in a number of ways in these verses.

1. The records are wiped clean

First, we discover that the record of our past lives is cancelled. Paul writes in verse 14 of **'the handwriting of requirements that was against us'**. The ESV describes this very effectively as 'the record of debt that stood against us with its legal demands'. Have we lived up to the standards that God has set? If a ledger was compiled on your life or mine using the principles of double-entry book-keeping, it would soon become clear that we were hopelessly in the red. The great evangelist George Whitefield described the spiritual crisis that marked his conversion as a time when he was always on edge, like a man afraid to look into his bank books in case it turned out that he was not solvent after all, but a bankrupt.

Nothing is more futile than trying to square accounts with God. Any sensitive soul who has ever tried it will discover, like Martin Luther, that the task is hopeless. But this is what forgiveness does. In a moment of high drama the records are wiped clean. All the incriminating evidence has been erased because our debt has been paid in full. Christ has offered his life to God in place of our failed lives and there is nothing left for us to pay. A forgiven man or woman has a record as clean as a whistle. That depressing catalogue of failure and sin is now blank. Every single entry has been deleted and nothing remains. If you are a Christian, there are no charges against your name. What could be better than that?

2. The record of our sins is nailed to the cross of Christ

Secondly, forgiveness means that the record of our past lives no longer applies to us. This is what Paul has in mind in verse 14 when he says that 'the handwriting' has been taken out of the way and nailed to the cross. It is possible that Paul was thinking here of one of the details of a typical crucifixion. It was Roman practice to pin a notice called the *'titulus'* to the cross above the condemned man's head. It gave the man's name and the crime that he was accused of. It was the proof that he was getting his just deserts. This very thing happened to Jesus. His name was affixed to the cross together with the explanation that he had claimed to be King of the Jews. In the same way, said Paul, it is as though the record of our past lives has been nailed to the cross where Jesus died. That being the case, it has nothing to do with us any more. Because it was fastened above his head it will never be nailed above ours. The Bible has other vivid ways of describing the same striking reality. Our sin is buried in the deepest part of the sea (Micah 7:19); it is irretrievable. It has been placed behind the back of God (Isa. 38:17); whichever way he turns, he cannot see it.

3. Christ has triumphed over the powers of evil

Thirdly, forgiveness means that the powers of evil are defeated foes. The language of verse 15 takes us back to ancient Rome, where a successful military campaign was always followed by a triumph. At the head of the parade came the victorious general, followed by his regiments in their best parade uniform. At the end came the prisoners of war, bedraggled and forlorn. The cheering crowds in Rome could enjoy a little glow of satisfaction. Was that pathetic specimen the mighty Caratacus[1] who had defied three whole legions? He was no threat to anyone now!

One thing that emerges from this letter is that the Colossians were obsessed with the unseen world. The new teachers offered advice on how to placate the dark forces. According to Paul, none of that was necessary. One of the most remarkable aspects of Jesus' crucifixion is that he **'disarmed principalities and powers'**, and **'made a public spectacle of them, triumphing over them in it'**. While the devil retains a certain limited freedom of movement, he is already a defeated foe. People who enjoy God's forgiveness should not be flippant about the Evil One. They should certainly pay him a healthy respect, but equally they should not react towards him with slavish fear.

Conclusion

Have you been converted? No one will ever ask you a more important question. If you have, do you appreciate what a great thing God has done for you? Think it over again and marvel at it. This should help you stop and think before you take on any modern versions of the teaching that troubled Paul, teachings that suggest that, even though you might be truly saved, the real blessing is not conversion but the next step, however that is conceived. Of course, there are blessings ahead. We are not in heaven yet and there is more to be known of God, even in this life, than any of us has yet grasped. But if we are Christians, the greatest blessing of all is ours already. There is nothing to equal conversion, no blessing that can surpass it. Don't rest for a moment until you know for a fact that you are a converted person, a true follower of Jesus.

And for those of us who are Christians already, whatever other blessings lie in store, God has already done by far the greater thing in giving us repentance and the faith to entrust ourselves to his Son. This side of heaven there is no greater miracle than the work of God in transforming human hearts and minds. High praise to the God who converts undeserving sinners into his adoring followers!

10.
Don't be intimidated!

Please read Colossians 2:16-17

According to the apostle Paul, every Christian is complete in Christ. There is every reason for the believer, whether in first-century Colosse or the rapidly changing world of the twenty-first century, to feel confident and positive. With such a great Saviour and such a great salvation, there is every reason to feel buoyant. In the light of this truth, it is sad to observe that Paul's first readers were having their confidence undermined, having come under the influence of teachers who agreed that we do indeed need faith in Christ, but claimed that saving faith of itself was not enough. According to these men, further insights, experiences and blessings were needed to fill out what was only a beginning. This situation explains Paul's instruction in verse 16: **'Let no one judge you.'** This forms the second of three stark warnings given in Colossians 2. In the same way, they must let no one take them captive (2:8) and let no one steal their spiritual treasure from under their noses (2:18).

'Judge' here means 'intimidate'. They must not let themselves become browbeaten or cowed. This alerts us to one of the problems at Colosse that prompted Paul to write. Any and every Christian is an extraordinary phenomenon. The work of grace in human hearts is so astounding that angels look on in wonderment. In Colosse, however, believers were being made to feel inferior. It would seem that the new teachers were always finding fault, which meant that church members were living under a cloud of disapproval. (Discipleship is hard work when you feel that you are always a disappointment to your leaders.) What form, then, did this fault-finding take?

Doing things they shouldn't (2:16)

One area where the newcomers judged the original members of the church to be deficient was in matters of **'food'** and **'drink'**. This suggests that they believed that the Old Testament dietary laws should be binding on all Christians. If anything, they went a step further. The Old Testament food laws said nothing at all about drink. A group known as the Nazirites abstained from alcohol, but this was entirely voluntary on their part. It seems likely that the members of the church in Colosse were being told that kosher food and teetotalism were both essential for godliness.

In short, the problem was a first-century form of a problem that reasserts itself at regular intervals in the history of the Christian church, namely legalism. The legalist is a person whose first response to a situation is to say within himself, 'What we need round here is some rules.' This of itself may not be a bad thing, but the legalist goes on to insist on rules that God does not insist upon. Every generation of Christians needs to ask the question: 'Whose rules are these?' To put it another way, 'Who is my master? Whom do I serve?' Anything that is commanded in the Word of God is binding on the conscience. Anything that is not found there cannot be applied with the same rigour.

None of this is to say that Paul did not give considerable support to the importance of self-discipline. For example, time slips through our fingers. We must redeem it (Eph. 5:16), find ways of buying it back so that those things that are truly important are not driven out of our lives and our schedules by things that are urgent but essentially trivial. Do we make time for God, time for prayer and Bible study? In the same way, the human body is an unruly bundle of appetites that need to be kept in check. Our ability to do so is one proof that our Christian profession is not just empty words (1 Cor. 9:27). It is always disturbing when a person who claims to be a Christian does not control his habits but is controlled by them. Imposing rules on ourselves can be a valuable aid to spiritual health. Imposing them on others, however, can be a form of tyranny.

In Romans 14 Paul makes the point that it is often an act of Christian love to defer to the scruples of others. In that chapter he fleshed this out with regard to two 'hot potatoes' of the day. One of them, as in Colosse, concerned the observance of special days (Rom. 14:5-6). The other concerned an issue that often arose for Christians converted against the backdrop of an overwhelmingly pagan culture: was it acceptable to eat meat that had already been offered to idols as part of pagan worship? With regard to both these issues, Paul made the point that it is not merely courteous but an act of love to curtail our freedom of action when that might cause unnecessary offence to another believer whose conscience is as yet somewhat immature. I may not share my brother's scruples and they may not be as biblically derived as he has tended to think, but it is neither kind nor helpful to flaunt my liberty and trample on his sensitive conscience.

In Romans 14 we meet the 'weaker brother', the Christian whose conscience is as yet ill-informed and hypersensitive. The situation in Colosse, however, was different. The people who were troubling the church members were not immature believers who had yet to learn how to think through their moral choices in a biblically informed manner. They were, in

fact, people with decided and settled convictions. The
'weaker brother' of Romans 14 is unsure of his ground and
feels threatened. The new teachers in Colosse knew exactly
where they stood and did the threatening. The Lord's people
were being cowed by those who usurped authority over their
consciences. Each man must stand or fall to his own master
(Rom. 14:4). Christ alone is Lord of the conscience and if
powerful figures in my personal world insist upon things
where he has remained silent, I have the right to demur.
'Stand fast therefore in the liberty by which Christ has made
us free, and do not be entangled again with a yoke of bondage' (Gal. 5:1).

Does this tussle in a first-century church have anything to
say to modern believers? Every generation of Christians
tends to develop a set of unwritten rules. They are often
largely negative. In effect, they are evangelical taboos. Do
these things, and you are written off as being worldly. When
I was a teenager, I can remember moving in Christian circles
where the older generation looked upon the youngsters'
enjoyment of films with instant and blanket disapproval.
Visit the cinema[1] and you had compromised your testimony,
no matter what was showing at the time. The most baffling
part of the whole thing was that you were expected to know
that such things were worldly without needing any explanation. At the same time, it can be genuinely difficult for a
certain type of Christian to see that what is a healthy discipline for him may not be so for everyone else. The continual
challenge before each generation of believers is to make sure
that we don't mistake the commands of Christ, which are
binding, for the evangelical version of the 'traditions of the
elders', which are at best voluntary.

Not doing what they should (2:16)

Christians in Colosse, as well as being chided for laxity over the Jewish food laws, were also being reproached for their failure to keep festivals, new moons and Sabbaths (2:16). Again this takes us back to the world of the Old Testament. Paul has lumped together in one phrase the whole Jewish calendar, with its observance of yearly feast days, monthly sacrifices and weekly Sabbaths. It is probable, however, that there was more at stake than a mere plea to reproduce the pattern of the Jewish religious year. Every culture has its seasonal rites of passage. Most of the believers in the Lycus Valley had emerged from a pagan thought world where it was assumed that seasonal rituals were also a way of paying due respect to the celestial powers that control the movement of the heavenly bodies, which in turn, have an impact on events on this earth. Were the newcomers advocating a blend where the outer framework of Jewish ritual catered for a mindset governed by assumptions that were actually pagan? This was one form of a process called syncretism.

Syncretism involves the fusion of different, even conflicting, elements of religious thought. It is still alive. Roman Catholicism has been very adept at imposing a Christian veneer on an underlying pagan culture. Many of the Andean peoples in Latin America still worship the old gods they served long before the Spaniards came, but for public consumption they have been given the names and outward identities of Catholic saints. In many parts of Africa, old pre-Christian customs persist. Born-again believers face considerable pressure to join in the rituals that set out to placate the spirits of departed ancestors. Syncretism is attractive essentially because it is a way of minimizing the collision of cultures that occurs when the claims of Christ come into conflict with the claims of religious, social and family tradition. It is, at heart, a way of modifying Christianity so as not to cause offence. Yet Jesus said, 'If anyone comes to me and does not hate his father and mother, wife and children, brothers and sisters, yes, and his own life also, he cannot be my disciple' (Luke 14:26).

In Colosse, the pattern was much the same as it had been over food laws. Believers were judged to have failed because they had not met a set of expectations that were not actually an essential part of Christian discipleship. As Christ's free men, they were entitled to ask their critics, 'Who has required this from your hand?' (Isa. 1:12). Followers of Jesus have enough to do complying with the commands that he has given. Teachers who insist on adding yet more obligations are like the scribes whom Jesus condemned for laying grievous and unnecessary burdens on people who had already had their quota of spiritual struggles (Luke 11:46).

Mistaking the shadow for the substance (2:17)

It is sad that the newcomers in Colosse made such an issue of observing the old Jewish festivals because these things had served their purpose but were now redundant. Paul expressed his concern at this point by making a telling contrast between the **'shadow'** and the **'substance'** (2:17). A shadow is, by its very nature, insubstantial. It only takes its shape from the solid object that casts it. But whereas a shadow is flimsy and ethereal, the substance is solid and tangible. In Paul's mind, the religious system of Israel prior to the coming of Christ was like a shadow — ephemeral and transient. The coming of Jesus, however, meant that the shadow had been replaced by the substance. That which was only ever meant to be temporary, because it was a pale silhouette of something much greater, should fade away. It has been eclipsed by the brilliant reality that it prefigured.

This idea is developed much more fully in the letter to the Hebrews, which is a sustained appeal to believers converted from a background in Judaism not to return to the old ways, for that would mean leaving the substance behind and returning to the world of half-light and shadows. One word that occurs again and again in Hebrews is the word 'better'. In Christ, the believer has a better high priest than the priests of Israel who offers a better sacrifice in a better sanctuary and so inaugurates a better covenant founded on better promises. The message of Hebrews is that a religious system that God himself had founded could now fade away. It was only ever meant to be preparatory and now it had served its purpose. Something glorious gave way to something clothed in the most excellent glory. The sacrificial system and priesthood were the shadow cast back in time by the Christ who had yet to come. Once he came, however, all the para-phernalia of the old system was redundant. Nevertheless, the psychological pull of the old ways was very strong for Jewish believers whose friends and families were still caught up in them.

Paul was dealing with a similar situation in Colosse. He wanted to provide ammunition for browbeaten Christians. Let them understand that those who wanted them to observe the traditional rituals of the Jewish year were majoring on minor issues. They should let the main thing be the main thing, and concentrate not on flimsy externals but the beauty, glory and sufficiency of Jesus Christ, priest and sacrifice for the people of God. The new teachers were making an enor-mous fuss about mere shadows, confusing the ephemeral with the solid and substantial, a transient and passing system with something permanent and enduring.

Conclusion

Two things arise from our consideration of this passage.

Firstly, to what extent do we allow our behaviour to be controlled by the expectations of people who are significant in our personal world? Sometimes new Christians yield to pressure from family members, loved ones and friends who are not themselves followers of Jesus. For the sake of avoiding conflict, there is the danger of allowing our personal agenda to be set by people other than Christ himself. The same thing can happen within the Christian community when believers allow their thinking to be shaped by powerful individuals who use guilt as a way of exacting compliance with their preferences. While we must certainly treat others with appropriate levels of tact and sensitivity, the believer's conscience must be captive to the Word of God.

Secondly, the danger of slipping back into the world of mere shadows is still with us. Millions of people today think that Christianity is a matter of priests conducting sacrifices on altars at the holy end of holy buildings. Christians who know their Bibles want nothing to do with this kind of thing. Our objection does not arise out of simple dislike for ornate premises, clothing and ceremony. Those who think in terms of a clerical priesthood conducting sacrifices have turned Paul's logic on its head, leaving the substance behind and embracing the shadows. Our objection to such thinking stems from our awe-struck sense of wonder at the greatness of Christ. He himself is all that Christian people could ever need in a priest. What are the priests of Christendom by comparison? His sacrifice is the only sacrifice necessary to bring sinners to God — a sacrifice so acceptable to God that it will never be repeated. There is no place now for the altar in the worship of Jesus. The priests, altars and sacrifices of Christendom are as redundant as those of ancient Israel.

11.
Don't let yourself be defrauded!

Please read Colossians 2:18-19

Have you ever been to any of the 'tube' stations on the central part of the London underground system? If so, you may have noticed warnings that say, 'Pickpockets operate in this station.' I have also noticed signs in some of the more remote car parks in the English Lake District advising walkers who are leaving their cars behind to lock everything out of sight in the boot. Thieves even operate at the top of the almost inaccessible Honister Pass! They are sometimes active around Christian churches too! This time I am not thinking so much of everyday burglars, who might try to lift communion plate or the offering box. The apostle Paul had in mind thieves who set out to steal something far more valuable than your wallet, or your credit and debit cards. In Colossians 2:18 he warned against believers being cheated or defrauded of their **'reward'**. In this case, 'reward' does not mean our reward in heaven, our salvation, but the full enjoyment of our faith as believers. There are shady operators who can rob a Christian of what is rightfully his. Yield an inch to them, and we may end up losing the joy in believing that is our due.

This warning was originally given to the members of a church in Colosse in Asia Minor in the first century. It forms

part of a wider pattern. Paul had also told them not to let
themselves be kidnapped (2:8) and not to be intimidated
(2:16). These repeated warnings all stemmed from the fact
that, as we have seen in earlier chapters, the fellowship in
Colosse had fallen prey to a group of new teachers whose
distinctive emphases were potentially very damaging to the
spiritual well-being of individual believers and the church as
a whole. At this point in his argument, Paul went on to
suggest that the newcomers were the spiritual equivalent of
burglars. While they claimed to enrich the believers in
Colosse, there was actually a real possibility that they would
impoverish them. A similar form of theft is still taking place
in today's Christian scene.

The burglar's technique (2:18)

Paul essentially accused the interlopers in Colosse of majoring on non-essentials, concentrating on lesser and external
matters to such an extent that the Christians there might lose
something far more important without noticing. They gave
enormous weight to things that did not concern the heart of
the gospel. Two things in particular stand out.

1. A bogus form of humility

The first is **'false humility'**. It goes without saying that the
truly humble man is not aware of his humility. Humility is
elusive. It is much easier to catch a red admiral butterfly in
one hand. Once we think we have attained it, we know we
haven't. Charles Dickens's character, Uriah Heap, is an
enjoyable literary creation. As soon as we hear him describe
himself as 'the 'umblest man around', we sense that he has
made himself look ridiculous. Yet, for all his absurdity, the
fact that he is continually prating about how ''umble' he is

tells us that his talk of humility is actually a way of directing attention to himself. In the same way, a Christian leader who invites others to think of him as a role model in humility is actually the very opposite. Remember that ' "God resists the proud, but gives grace to the humble." Therefore humble yourselves under the mighty hand of God, that he may exalt you in due time' (1 Peter 5:5-6).

Even so, I think that here in Colossians 2:18 Paul has more in mind than just a generalized warning about the dangers of a pretended humility with no substance behind it. It is likely that the newcomers in Colosse were advocating a particular kind of 'humility', and for a particular reason. Some commentators suggest that the Greek word translated **'humility'** has connotations of asceticism, or self-denial, with particular reference to fasting. If that view is correct, the newcomers had told the believers in Colosse that they needed to humble themselves by taking up the path of self-denial. This would be a necessary prelude for a special experience of enlightenment. Going without food would make them receptive to the blessing that God has in store for those who are willing to take the path of restraint and moderation.

It would be easy to see why believers could be taken in by this line of reasoning. There is a genuine strand of Christian teaching that emphasizes both self-discipline and authentic meekness. There is a degree of truth in the saying, 'The way down is the way up.' The new teachers, however, were advocating a bogus form of humility. The classic problem of asceticism is that the focus is all on externals — such things as how much I go without during Lent, or the bleeding feet of pilgrims who have made the ascent of Croagh Patrick[1] barefoot. It becomes a way of accumulating merit. Depriving the body of pleasures may have some limited value in teaching it who is master, but the real work has to be done on what we are inside. The best advice for believers, then and now, is not so much to keep a diet, but: 'Keep your heart with all diligence, for out of it spring the issues of life' (Prov. 4:23).

2. The 'worship of angels'

Paul also noted that the spiritual burglars in Colosse made much of the **'worship of angels'**. Does this mean that they were advocating that the angels should be worshipped? If so, this would be very serious indeed. For a professing Christian to worship the Holy Trinity on the one hand, while also worshipping angels on the other, would imply that there were other mediators between God and man than the Lord Jesus Christ alone. The practice of offering worship to angelic beings did indeed become a problem in this region some centuries later. A synod was held in Laodicea in AD 363, which decreed, 'It is not right for Christians to abandon the church of God and go away to invoke angels.' Having said that, I am not certain that this is what Paul had in mind. He wrote at an early period in the history of the Christian church, probably too early for a serious error that taught that angels could be worshipped alongside, and in addition to, the one true God revealed in Scripture to have taken a hold.

By 'worship of angels' I suspect that Paul meant 'the kind of worship that the angels offer', 'worship angel style'. This would fit in with the kind of elitism that the newcomers favoured. They would suggest, in effect, that we cannot expect to be truly blessed until we worship as the angels do. While we cannot be certain, this may have involved learning a type or style of singing, perhaps tied in with a kind of ecstatic speech, on the grounds that they were singing in 'the tongues ... of angels' (1 Cor. 13:1).

I don't know whether any groups of twenty-first-century Christians argue that we should copy the worship style of the angels, but in a more general sense, worship is a bone of contention among modern believers. It is not unusual for Christians to conclude that they have embraced a superior approach to worship than that chosen by others. Their style and ethos is Spirit-filled, while others, by comparison, are dead and lifeless. Churches are judged and pigeonholed according to the externals of worship, and unfavourable comparisons can be made in both directions. Paul wanted his readers to understand that an excessive preoccupation with such outward matters could only detract in the long run from much more central issues, yet over the years believers have proved very adept at censuring the worship of others because of trifles. Baptists in the late nineteenth century thoroughly disapproved of those chapels that installed pipe organs. (This was seen at that time and in that setting as 'the first step on the slippery slope'.) Nowadays you can be written off if there is not a drum kit alongside the pulpit. ('Those guys are stuck in a time warp.')

The use or non-use of a prayer book, or the presence of absence in the service of open prayer, can bring down the same kind of disapproval from those who do things differently. Yet which of us can read the hearts of those worshippers whose style is different from our own? Charles Simeon had a note in his pulpit, which read, 'Humble the sinner, exalt the Saviour and promote holiness.' He majored on the things that really mattered. We would do well to imitate him rather than the burglars of Colosse.

The burglar's authority (2:18)

The NKJV translation of this verse speaks of someone **'intruding into those things which he has not seen'**. Incidentally, Paul's use of the word **'he'** at this point has led some to wonder whether he had one particular teacher in mind. There is also a vigorous debate as to whether English translations of the Bible should include the word '**not**' at this point. Some ancient texts do not include it. If we were to follow them, the problem would lie not so much with what the man has *not* seen as with what he *has* seen. This is why the ESV speaks of someone 'going on in detail about visions'. In short, this man did not derive his teaching from Scripture alone, but claimed direct revelation from God.

This is a problem that has resurfaced at regular intervals in church history. Very soon after Martin Luther brought the Reformation to Wittenberg, he was faced with a takeover bid from a number of teachers called the 'Zwickau prophets'. One of the most outspoken of this group was a man named Thomas Münzer, who argued that Luther had got rid of one pope and replaced him with another, a pope made of paper. Luther in turn was robustly dismissive of Münzer's claims to direct revelations from the Spirit, telling him, 'I slap your spirit on the snout.' It would do us good to remind ourselves that the Holy Spirit has gone into print. There need be no misunderstanding or ambiguity.

Sadly, Thomas Münzer has his modern equivalents. I remember seeing a book on sale at a Christian event in the early 1970s called *The Vision*. It was written by a prominent evangelical leader of the day[2] and gave a detailed description of a number of things that he expected to see happen within the next ten years. Not long ago, I was preaching at a Christian Union meeting at a university in the north-west of England when a young man told me, face aglow, of certain prophecies that he had heard.

I am sure that some who hold that God speaks directly and bypasses the Bible mean well and simply cannot see where their logic is taking them. Paul, none the less, saw this as the domain of the spiritual pickpocket. Guide people away from the Bible, and vagueness, and even fantasy, takes the place of clarity. Christians today need to be especially on the alert in this area since the Bible is increasingly downplayed even in churches that once had a good name for expounding it. When the Bible is explained, God speaks. Move away from expounding Scripture, and the voice of God is heard progressively less often. The man who will explain the Word of God to you is your friend. Spiritual leaders who shun Holy Scripture deserve to be avoided like the plague.

The burglar's character (2:18-19)

1. He presents an over-inflated image of himself

Paul told his readers that the intruders who troubled the church in Colosse were **'puffed up'**. There are some species of frogs that have the power to inflate themselves by way of rapid breathing in order to frighten off predators. Of course, the bloated amphibian is not really as big as it looks. The intimidating display is all pretence. And the hyper-inflated authority figure in some churches is not in fact as considerable as he seems. It is 'vain'. There is no real justification for the swollen image he presents, for it has no real substance behind it. The emperor isn't wearing any clothes.

2. He is not holding fast to Christ

A further problem with this kind of person in Colosse was that he was not as focused on God as he liked to think. His mind was dominated by ways of thinking that would be normal outside the church. In consequence, he was **'not holding fast to the Head'**. Until quite recently I was involved each summer in helping at a Christian camp for teenagers. My main responsibility was to provide the Bible teaching, but as I used to enjoy outdoor sports I also lent a hand with some of the activities. Teaching young people rock-climbing has its amusing moments. In moments of panic they will sometimes grab hold of anything at all other than the rock — the instructor's legs, the rope, or even flimsy daisies growing out of crevices on the crag. The trouble is that you can only get hold of these things by letting go of the one thing that can guarantee your security — the rock itself. In the same way, major on non-essentials and your grip on Christ himself will become weakened. This is not the way things ought to be.

The church in Colosse is portrayed here as a **'body, nourished and knit together by joints and ligaments'**. When, however, some parts of the body maintain their close connection with the head and others do not, the internal cohesion of the church begins to suffer. The rest of the 'body' is joined first and foremost to Christ. If our grip on him lessens, our closeness to those others who are also joined to him will suffer.

Conclusion

If one message emerges from this passage it is surely that we should be on our guard against the burglars and pickpockets of the spiritual realm. Among other things, this will involve learning how to spot them. We should be particularly on our guard when spiritual leaders focus on relatively minor matters of Christian conduct while at the same time neglecting the central teachings of the faith and the place that Christ should occupy in all our devotion.

Caution is also needed when those in authority seem to be leading people away from the Bible, partly by departing from its teaching in subtle ways, and partly by paying less attention to it as a whole than Christians of a former generation. Spiritual leaders of this kind rob their people blind because they deprive them of contact with the Head of the church. Ignorance of the Bible always results in ignorance of

Christ, and if those who are called to be preachers pay increasingly little attention to Scripture, the people who listen to them will find that, by slow stages, Christ will become distant and remote. This will bring other miserable consequences with it.

Let spiritual burglars deprive you of your grasp on Christian essentials, and your walk with God will suffer, and so will your enjoyment of Christian fellowship. Fellowship is always at its sweetest and deepest when our relationship with the 'Head' is as it ought to be.

12.
Why do Christians let the world set their agenda?

Please read Colossians 2:20-23

So far, most of Colossians 2 has been taken up with warning the believers in Colosse what would happen if they gave a hearing to the newcomers who claimed to offer a more sophisticated and fulfilling version of Christianity.

First of all, they could be 'cheated' (2:8), taken captive by a set of opinions that were not actually Christ's gospel at all. Secondly, there was a real danger that they could be 'judged' (2:16), that harsh spiritual critics would browbeat them with the allegation that their discipleship was inadequate because they did not follow the regulations that the new teachers demanded. Finally, Paul warned the believers in Colosse that they might lose something precious (2:18). The new teachers meant to rob them of their enjoyment of Christ and replace it with a flimsy, bogus and inferior spirituality.

Now, in the last few verses of the chapter (2:20-23), Paul brought his warnings to a conclusion. He did so by posing a searching question that was intended to remind the Christians at Colosse of just how much was at stake should they throw in their lot with the false teachers. The thrust of that question is: 'Given that you no longer belong to the world outside the church, why live by its standards?' There is no doubt that Paul deserves a careful hearing from modern

Christians. Churches are still being seduced from first principles and stolen from under the noses of their members.

Submitting to the world's gospel makes no sense (2:20)

The main thrust of this verse is a pungent question intended to make Christians who were in danger of having their church stolen sit up and take notice: **'Why ... do you subject yourselves to regulations?'** The new teachers imposed a code of conduct on their followers. Believers in Colosse were being enticed to fall in with these demands. Perhaps some had already given way. Paul wanted them to understand that it was completely inappropriate for a Christian to submit to a set of regulations imposed by anyone other than Christ himself. Something is true of every Christian that means that he is under no obligation to any set of principles, any spiritual powers, or any earthly teacher beyond the allegiance that he already owes to Christ. As Christ's free man (or woman), no other claim on the believer's loyalty should be entertained for a moment. Christ alone is Lord of the conscience.

1. Hidden powers were at work

In the case of those first-century believers in Colosse, the rival to Christ was what Paul called **'the basic principles of the world'**. We have already met this phrase in verse 8, where we noted that there is a difference of opinion among Bible-believing scholars as to how it should be translated. If the NKJV is correct, Paul was saying that the teaching of the newcomers was rudimentary. Its origin was not in what Jesus taught, but in the 'world'; in other words, these were the kind of opinions that arise among men who will not submit to God. Far from being advanced teaching for the spiritually sophisticated, it was all very elementary and basic.

However, as we saw in that earlier passage, there is good reason to understand Paul to be saying that the teaching of these men was according to the 'elemental spirits'. There are powers at work that we cannot see, powers that influence the minds of people without their knowing it. Paul, writing to Timothy, speaks of those who give 'heed to deceiving spirits and doctrines of demons' (1 Tim. 4:1). It is sobering to reflect that the religious convictions of a large proportion of mankind are actually shaped and moulded by invisible but malicious intelligences bent on leading people away from God.

2. The Christian is dead to these things

Paul wanted his readers in Colosse to understand that these things have no claim on the believer because each and every Christian has **'died with Christ'**. We meet this idea elsewhere in Paul's writings. In Galatians 2:20 the apostle stated that he was no longer the person he had once been because he had been 'crucified with Christ'. There is a more extended treatment of the same idea in Romans 6:1-10, where Paul argues that sin once reigned over us just as a cruel tyrant oppresses his unfortunate subjects. There is no need, however, for a Christian to respond to the promptings of his former ruler, for he has 'died to sin' (Rom. 6:2), and all obligations cease with death. Believers are 'in Christ'. Jesus has identified so closely with his people that their standing and their destiny are inextricably linked with his. When Christ died there is a sense in which the believer died with him and is now a new person altogether.

My father died in 1971. Since that time he has not paid a penny in taxes. In the event of a war he will not be called up to serve with HM forces. The British Crown has no claim on his loyalty or his money. As a citizen of a much better world than this one, he is now outside the queen's jurisdiction, and laws passed by the Parliament in Westminster no longer impinge on him. In the same way, the 'basic principles', whether we regard them as the attitudes that are typical of unconverted people or the dark forces that mould the minds of men, have no claim on the believer. The person that I now am was not born within their territory.

To sum up so far, given that the Christian has ceased to live under the sway of these things, because the person that he once was no longer exists and he is a new person altogether, it is absurd and irrational for him to go on living like an unconverted person, as though the things that once controlled him still had a right to do so. And this is not simply an issue that belongs in the first century. The force of Paul's logic is still devastating. If I really am a new person I should be different. A clean break with the past and with the world at large is called for.

The world's rules make no sense (2:21-22)

The new teachers in Colosse encouraged a religion of self-denial and abstinence. The list of prohibitions in verse 21 (**'Do not touch, do not taste, do not handle'**) shows us their ideal for the truly enlightened man. He would abstain from certain foodstuffs and pleasures.

This kind of outlook is common in many religions. The orthodox Jew is kosher. The Muslim abstains from eating pork and will not touch alcohol (though this never seems to prevent Muslim shopkeepers from selling large quantities of it to their infidel customers!). The Mormon will not drink tea or coffee. Buddhist monks are forbidden to sleep on luxurious beds, handle money, eat food after midday, indulge in entertainments, or wear ornaments or perfumes. This mentality is so pervasive that many people automatically assume that any religion is basically about going without pleasures and

imposing austerities on ourselves. Roman Catholics do
without various things during Lent. In their circles it is also
assumed that those who have a religious vocation must make
a vow of perpetual celibacy.

Of course, it suits the enemy to present religion in this
kind of light. This is, firstly, because a religion of rules
distracts people from the true heart of Christianity, which is a
personal relationship with Christ and a life-changing experience of his grace, his wonderful kindness to the undeserving.
Secondly, it appeals to something in human nature. When the
Holy Spirit goes to work in a human life, his grace will
eventually disarm us. Our instinctive reaction, however, is to
resist grace. We resent it because it operates on the assumption that we are undeserving sinners who need God's forgiveness. We prefer the idea that the way to God should be
based on merit. It flatters our sense of ourselves.

1. Externals are of no lasting value

Paul goes on to insist that not only is a religion that is based
on rules not authentic Christianity, but it does not even make
sense. In the first place, this is because it concerns things
'which perish with the using' (2:22). We cannot build for
eternity by investing in perishable things a degree of significance that goes far beyond their actual importance.

This was Jesus' logic in Matthew 15:17, where he challenged the assumption of the Pharisees that a person can be
morally and spiritually defiled by certain foodstuffs: 'Do you
not yet understand that whatever enters the mouth goes into
the stomach and is eliminated?' After our food has been
digested, what is left is expelled from our bodies. In the
meantime, it is a mistake to think that something so basic has
affected our relationship with God on its way through the
alimentary canal. We should be far more concerned about
what is already inside us: 'Those things which proceed out of

the mouth come from the heart, and they defile a man. For out of the heart proceed evil thoughts, murders, adulteries, fornications, thefts, false witnesses, blasphemies. These are the things which defile a man...' (Matt. 15:18-20). By all means eat halal meat or be a vegetarian if you must, but neither course of action will affect your soul. The religions of this world are often obsessed with external things; Jesus is more concerned about what we are like at heart.

2. The rules are man-made

Paul goes on to give a second reason why a religion based on rules defies all logic. The rules are man-made. They are **'according to the commandments and doctrines of men'** (2:22). Why should we pay any attention to rules that our Saviour himself does not insist upon? Isaiah's question, quoted earlier, is still pertinent: 'Who has required this from your hand?' (Isa. 1:12). It is noticeable that, as Eastern religions have taken hold in the West, there has been a proliferation of teachers, masters, gurus, and so on. The Christian is answerable to his own Master, and to no one else.

Another striking difference can be observed between the things that Jesus requires of his followers and the man-made rules of much religion. When we are at our best, it is no chore to fall in with the wishes of someone who gave his life for us. Love and gratitude are so overwhelming that we would willingly do anything for one who died in our place. But, like the Pharisees, those who devise elaborate codes of regulations cripple their followers under the sheer weight of them: 'They bind heavy burdens, hard to bear, and lay them on men's shoulders' (Matt. 23:4).

The world's rules will only make things worse (2:23)

There is no doubt that a religion of taboos and self-imposed privations can be attractive. Paul conceded that people are impressed by that kind of thing. It has **'an appearance of wisdom'**. At best, however, it is **'self-imposed religion'**, or as the AV puts it, 'will worship'. Those who practise it are enslaving their consciences to their own religious fantasies. Nevertheless, others can be taken in because, on the face of it, discipline and self-sacrifice appear to be at the forefront. Onlookers conclude that someone has paid a heavy price for his enlightenment in terms of the **'neglect of the body'**. If someone has gone without certain pleasures and denied himself the fulfilment of legitimate appetites, if he has borne pain, discomfort and inconvenience, there will always be some who are ready to conclude that they are in the presence of a spiritual giant.

At this point a note of caution would be appropriate. As we saw earlier, there is a place for self-denial in the Christian life. Paul wrote elsewhere of disciplining his body and bringing it 'into subjection' (1 Cor. 9:27). He did not allow his physical appetites to gain the upper hand. He showed his physical constitution who was master for the sake of being an efficient and productive servant of Christ. It is quite a different matter, however, to suppose that these disciplines are themselves the way to eternal life.

Another danger occurs when we take a discipline that has proved wholesome and effective in our own case and make it a universal rule for everyone else to follow. 'Who are you to judge another's servant? To his own master he strands or falls' (Rom. 14:4).

Paul wanted his readers to understand, however, that the most damaging aspect of a religion of man-made rules is that it cannot achieve its object. Such rules **'are of no value against the indulgence of the flesh'**. They cannot conquer the tendency of the flesh to indulge its appetites. By **'the flesh'** Paul does not so much mean our physical bodies as the unregenerate nature, with its selfish appetites and desires. Either we are governed by the Holy Spirit of God, or we are dominated by 'the flesh'. There is a terrible irony here. The new teachers at Colosse were urging their followers to adopt all sorts of rules on the basis that this would help them to curb their innate capacity for self-pleasing and self-worship. Paul insisted, however, that keeping such man-made rules would only feed the very appetites they hoped to restrain. Attain a high standard in keeping regulations and observing taboos, and it will pander to your pride. Inevitably, you feel pleased with yourself and confident in your moral performance. Nothing could be more disastrous when the very thing that we most need is to learn how to despair of ourselves and put our whole trust in Christ.

Conclusion

We have in this passage a telling contrast between religion and Christianity. Mere religion can never be enough for a follower of Jesus. As people who have undergone a dramatic change, a change so marked that it can only be understood as a spiritual death and rebirth, the unseen powers that concoct the world's philosophies and religious systems have nothing to say to us. The rules that they devise can never address the central problem of the human condition, the rebellious and self-satisfied heart, and, in the end, religion is counterproductive. Far from humbling human hearts and teaching us to place all our confidence in Christ, it encourages us to place our confidence in our own spiritual attainments.

13.
Be heavenly-minded!

Please read Colossians 3:1-4

What kind of people does our society most need? What kind of person is most likely to make an impact in today's world? According to our passage, the answer is something of a paradox. The people who will do most good are the kind who don't really belong. In modern English the word 'alien' often has sinister connotations, but the people who will make a difference in any culture or era of history will always have an alien quality about them. They will never really fit in. They will seem like visitors from a world that is decidedly 'other' and much better than this one. Simply by being themselves they will challenge the people and the values of contemporary society.

'Be what you are' (3:1)

The apostle Paul wanted his first readers in first-century Colosse to realize that, in this world, Christians are indeed a kind of resident alien. Their real identity and origin are not earthly, but heavenly. As physical organisms we were born in this world but, having 'died with Christ' (2:20), we no longer belong to it. A second, spiritual birth means that our true citizenship is in heaven and something of the quality of that place ought to cling to us even as we live out our days in this present world. The world needs heavenly people as never before, and this is what Christians are when they live up to their true identity. The message of this passage to Christians, whether in the first or twenty-first century, then, is: 'Be what you are!'

In every age and culture, certain things follow from the fact that each believer has been **'raised with Christ'** (3:1). (In the NKJV verse 1 opens with **'If'**. This carries the sense of 'Since you were raised with Christ ...,' or 'Given that you were raised with Christ...') We have already met this idea in Colossians 2. It stems from Paul's teaching in a number of places that each Christian is a person 'in Christ'. In the mind of God, the Christian is so closely identified with his Saviour that his standing, his destiny and his very identity are inextricably linked to Jesus. Thus, when Jesus died at Calvary, there is a sense in which the person that the believer used to be prior to his conversion died with him, and that person no longer exists. The Christian is no longer under the dominion of sin, the most cruel tyrant ever to enslave men and women (Rom. 6:6-7); nor is he any longer under the control of the elemental powers, those hidden forces that influence the majority of people without their knowing it (2:20). Instead, 'If anyone is in Christ, he is a new creation; old things have passed away; behold, all things have become new' (2 Cor. 5:17). Each believer has been raised with Christ 'in the likeness of his resurrection' (Rom. 6:5), 'raised with him [i.e. Christ] through faith in the working of God, who raised him from the dead' (2:12). To be 'raised with Christ' is to have undergone a joint resurrection with him.

Thus Paul had something thrilling to say to Christians who were being enticed by the idea that they needed something more than normal Christianity. But how can we improve on the wonderful fact that, although physically

Christians are still on earth, spiritually speaking, their birth was heavenly, their standing and their blessings are in heaven (Eph. 1:3) and heaven is their ultimate destination? In calling upon Christians to be what they are, Paul set before the Colossians the challenge to live as heavenly people and, in doing so, to bring something of the quality of heaven to earth to irradiate and suffuse all their relationships and life situations. Some Christians have certainly achieved this. The Puritan Richard Sibbes,[1] the Covenanter Samuel Rutherford[2] and Robert Murray M'Cheyne[3] in nineteenth-century Scotland all brought the glow of heaven to this broken world and made it much the better for their passing. The world still needs people like that.

Something to look for (3:1)

Those who have been raised with Christ must **'seek those things which are above'**. Only a person who has died and been born again can do that. It is a very persistent cliché in Christian circles to refer to people who have not yet come to faith in Christ as 'seekers'. This is not a biblically informed way to describe such people. Paul writes elsewhere that, by nature, 'There is none who seeks after God' (Rom. 3:11). If anything, rather than searching for God, unbelievers run away from him and search for excuses. Some go looking for miraculous signs, while others seek wisdom (1 Cor. 1:22), but this is often a ploy to avoid real contact with God. Ever since the first man hid himself in the garden and God came looking for him, mankind has been lost. It is God who does the seeking. For those who are trying to hide, spirituality can be a very effective smokescreen. But once a person has been taught by grace to value Christ, he will seek more contact with him.

Incidentally, it is also worth noting that Paul did not encourage his readers to 'seek those things which are within'. It is often supposed that the way to enlightenment involves looking inside ourselves. The way of the mystic can seem very attractive. But the only light that it offers is like those lanterns that used to be hung out on the cliff tops of the Cornish coast by wreckers to lure ships into danger.[4] That way lies shipwreck. The human heart, human instincts and motives have all been fatally skewed by the Fall. There is no hope of spiritual enlightenment or safety for those who go looking in that direction. We must steer our course in the direction of the only true and safe light, 'where Christ is'. In the Greek, the verb translated **'seek'** means that we are to seek continually, with determination and consistency. Sporadic and fitful seeking will not suffice.

And what are we to seek?

1. We seek Christ

First of all, we are to seek Christ himself. In effect, Paul told his readers that they must follow hard after Jesus and pursue him relentlessly, never letting him out of their sight. We must not allow our relationship with him to flag, or lose its intensity, but must keep in constant touch with him.

2. We seek what pleases Christ

This means in second place that we must also seek the things that please him. To go after things that displease him will only alienate him, so believers must make it their business to pursue the values and behaviour that pertain to his kingdom. What does this involve? Paul gives us an outline of Christian character in action later in the chapter: 'Therefore, as the elect of God, holy and beloved, put on tender mercies, kindness, humility, meekness, longsuffering; bearing with one another, and forgiving one another, if anyone has a complaint against another; even as Christ forgave you, so you also must do. But above all these things put on love, which is the bond of perfection. And let the peace of God rule in your hearts, to which also you were called in one body; and be thankful. Let the word of Christ dwell in you richly in all wisdom, teaching and admonishing one another in psalms and hymns and spiritual songs, singing with grace in your hearts to the Lord. And whatever you do in word or deed, do all in the name of the Lord Jesus, giving thanks to God the Father through him' (3:12-17).

3. We seek a living, reigning King

Paul goes on to strike a note of reassurance by pointing out that the Christ whom we seek is **'sitting at the right hand of God'** (3:1). There is an echo here of Psalm110:1:

> The LORD said to my Lord,
> 'Sit at my right hand,
> Till I make your enemies your footstool.'

In that psalm, David speaks of someone whom he calls 'my Lord' whom God rewards with a place at his right hand, a royal conqueror exalted to the highest place after a crushing victory over his foes. God's Messiah is enthroned in the place of victory, authority and power. The Christ whom we are to seek is not a dead prophet but a reigning sovereign, the King of Kings and Lord of Lords.

When Peter and John were put on trial before the Sanhedrin, the highest court in ancient Israel, for preaching the gospel, they made a profound impression on the assembled judges: 'Now when they saw the boldness of Peter and John, and perceived that they were uneducated and untrained men, they marvelled. And they realized that they had been with

Jesus' (Acts 4:13). In the same way, if we 'seek those things which are above' consistently and wholeheartedly, people around us ought to be thinking, 'There's something about those people.'

Something to think about (3:2-3)

Paul's next exhortation to the Colossian believers was that they should take control of their thought lives. These are to be redirected. We are no longer to let ourselves become preoccupied with 'the things of earth', the things that came naturally when our horizon was no higher than the rim of this world, with its achievements, rewards and pleasures, but to set our minds **'on things above'**.

One of the benefits of buying a computer with a powerful processor is that it will be capable of multitasking, performing several operations at the same time. But in the end a computer is only a machine, a box containing a silicon chip and masses of circuitry. Bible concordance software will not make the machine healthier, any more than Internet pornography will harm it. The human mind, however, was designed by a holy God. Our powers of thought were intended to be used for his glory and there are ways of thinking that threaten our well-being. And we cannot multitask. Our minds cannot think about Christ and sin at one and the same time, not without threatening our sanity. Jesus said, 'No one can serve two masters; for either he will hate the one and love the other, or else he will be loyal to the one and despise the other. You cannot serve God and mammon' (Matt. 6:24). In the same way, allowing our minds to dwell on things that are evil will drive out thoughts about the unsearchable riches of Christ, whereas training ourselves to think about Jesus and his love will have the positive effect of driving away the kind of thoughts that dishonour him and us. Nothing gets rid of mental pollutants more effectively than meditating on the perfections of our Saviour and his love for his people. If, for instance, we steel ourselves by saying, 'I will not think about sin,' sin remains at the forefront of our minds. The mind is never a vacuum and it is never neutral. There is wisdom in the old chorus:

> Turn your eyes upon Jesus,
> Look full in his wonderful face.
> And the things of earth will grow strangely dim,
> In the light of his glory and grace.

On a practical note, we should also observe that the phrase **'set your mind'** describes a continuous activity. We are to make a habit of directing our thinking away from sin and towards Christ. Don't stop and don't give up!

Paul goes on to give a tremendous incentive for cultivating a heavenly mindset. Since Christians have died with Christ, although our physical bodies are still here, our life is not. It is **'hidden with Christ in God'** (3:3). This delightful and heart-warming phrase is well worth exploring. It is worth noting three levels of meaning.

1. The believer's union with Christ

In the first place, the Christian life is a life **'with Christ'**. He is the source of it. His risen life is now ours. This is what Paul had in mind when he wrote elsewhere, 'I have been crucified with Christ; it is no longer I who live, but Christ lives in me; and the life which I now live in the flesh I live by faith in the Son of God, who loved me and gave himself for me' (Gal. 2:20). The believer's life is lived in partnership with Jesus and in the closest proximity to him. It is the kind of life that could only be extinguished if Jesus Christ himself could be snuffed out. That is why Paul could write as he did in Romans 8:38-39: 'For I am persuaded that neither death nor life, nor angels nor principalities nor powers, nor things present nor things to come, nor height nor depth, nor any other created thing, shall be able to separate us from the love of God which is in Christ Jesus our Lord.'

2. The believer's life is not of this world

Secondly, this life is **'hidden with Christ in God'**. Its location is not earthly but heavenly. It belongs elsewhere. Its home is in the mind and heart of God and it is not accessible to the human understanding, for a life that is hidden cannot be seen. The true identity of Christian people has yet to be revealed to the world at large. In the meantime, the whole of creation 'eagerly waits' to discover the glorious reality (Rom. 8:19). To people who are not Christians, the whole thing is a mystery. They know nothing of the divine origins of a Christian's life; their eyes are closed to a whole dimension of existence that can only be perceived through faith. Indeed, they are blind to the great reality of Jesus himself. The Christian is, as Thoreau said, marching to the beat of a different drummer. Believers, whether in New Testament times or today, have been won over and captivated by someone they cannot see, are taking directions from an unseen HQ, are loyal to an unseen land and are heading with anticipation towards an unseen destination.

3. The believer's life is secure from all harm

Thirdly, we should note that a hidden life is safe. Nothing can harm it. Enemies cannot locate the source of our life because it is hidden within the very being of God. A life that has been lodged for safe keeping within God himself is secure against all threats. Many years ago, I read a thrilling book by a Dutch lady, Corrie Ten Boom, called *The Hiding*

Place. It tells the story of her teenage years in Utrecht, in the Netherlands, when, during the Second World War, her family hid Jewish refugees from the Gestapo. Sadly, the Germans eventually located the refugees and the family was carted off to a concentration camp along with them. Although the family suffered terrible privations, the Christian testimony of its members never wavered. The real story of the book was not so much that of a physical hideaway where refugees could be concealed, but of a hiding place close to the heart of God, a shelter for the soul that is beyond the reach of harm. All believers have access to such a refuge. Enemies cannot find it and we cannot be dragged away from it. This is why many Christians down the years have faced martyrdom with serene courage. The enemies of the gospel can torture, even destroy, our bodies, but the life that we have is 'hidden with Christ in God'. It is completely out of their reach.

Something to look forward to (3:4)

This letter is full of Christ. As we have seen, this emphasis is necessary because the Colossian believers were in danger of accepting a spiritual package that would fob them off with a diminished Jesus. The new teachers argued that they would not have Christianity of the highest order unless they added various things to the gospel that Epaphras had introduced to their town. But if, as these newcomers said, we are not complete until we have added to Christ such things as spiritual experiences and encounters with spiritual powers, or if, as some say nowadays, the 'full gospel' is about Christ plus experiences and gifts, we have inevitably robbed Christ of his rightful place in a believer's estimation because we have said that he, by himself, is not enough. (Samuel Rutherford said of Christ that 'He is his lone self a sufficient heaven.') This is why Paul stated with childlike simplicity, **'Christ ... is our life'** (3:4). Jesus is the pearl of great price, the Rose of Sharon, the lily of the valley, the fairest of ten thousand. Superlatives die on our tongues when we try to describe him. Language dries up. There are no words to describe him. His beauty goes far beyond the power of the most copious and precise vocabulary. We are left stammering: 'For to me, to live is Christ, and to die is gain' (Phil. 1:21). No man or woman could do anything better or finer with a life than to spend it in the service of such a King.

And, more wonderful still, a hidden Saviour is to appear, and all his people will appear with him. At present a Christian's lot is misunderstanding, misrepresentation, scorn, and often much worse. We can look forward, however, to a day of vindication. The followers of Jesus, derided by those who are blind to unseen realities, will share his triumph: 'Beloved, now we are children of God; and it has not yet been revealed what we shall be, but we know that when he is revealed, we shall be like him, for we shall see him as he is' (1 John 3:2).

Conclusion

We have in this passage at one and the same time a stiff challenge and a wonderful incentive. On the one hand, we are called to rein in our stubborn thought lives, to take control of the inner world, directing it away from all that is unworthy and focusing it on Christ. This is no easy matter, but in case we are tempted to quail at the challenge, on the other hand we have the spur of knowing that our spiritual status and our future will not allow us to settle for anything less. Whatever the location of our physical bodies, our real lives are 'where Christ is' (3:1), in safe keeping with a Saviour beyond the reach of his foes. We also have a cast-iron guarantee that when he returns to this world to make all things new, we 'also will appear with him in glory' (3:4). In view of what grace has made us and the certainty of a glorious future, what else can we do but 'seek those things which are above'?

14.
Take no prisoners!

Please read Colossians 3:5-11

Setting the scene (3:5)

Something stands out as we read this section. The tone is set by a clear, ringing command. The apostle Paul wanted his readers in first-century Colosse to do something. It was a task that called for a ruthless streak, but it was straightforward: **'Put to death your members which are on the earth.'** The Greek verb behind the phrase **'put to death'** is strong and forceful. Something dangerous is on the loose. Every Christian needs to be on his guard against it because it is life-threatening. It means us nothing but harm.

I used to work with a man who took part in the D-Day landings in Normandy in June 1944. He was a soldier in one of the Highland regiments. In the fierce fighting around the city of Caen he came face to face with a German soldier. Each man now had an opportunity to practise his bayonet drill, not against a sack stuffed with straw but against a living, breathing enemy bent on his destruction. The boy in the kilt won.[1] The bayonet on the end of his Lee-Enfield rifle went home with such force that he could only extract it by firing a round into his opponent's body. It was a matter of kill or be killed. In the same way, Paul wanted his readers to grasp the fact that each Christian must steel himself to the ruthless extermination of spiritual foes that would, given the chance, destroy him.

1. Reigning and remaining sin

The Christian's mortal foe is described in verse 5 as **'your members which are on the earth'**. Some readers may detect a problem at this point. Paul has already said that each and every Christian 'has died with Christ' (2:20) — in other words, that the person that he or she once was has ceased to exist. In that case, what is left that needs killing? Any thoughtful believer knows that there is something inside him that refuses to lie down and die. So, if I have been 'crucified with Christ' (Gal. 2:20), why is temptation so persistent and so intense? It is important to note that Paul writes about our relationship to sin in two ways.

In the first place, he writes about it as though it were *an evil tyrant who once ruled over us*. We used to be the 'slaves of sin' (Rom. 6:6), but because our 'old man', the person that each of us used to be before we became Christians, is dead, we are his slaves no longer. His hideous majesty King Sin can make no legitimate claim on us. Having died, we are no longer under his jurisdiction. This is what the Puritans called 'reigning sin', and sin's reign is over. It no longer has dominion over the believer (Rom. 6:14). That does not mean, however, that sin has nothing to do with the Christian at all.

In second place, Paul noted that, though no longer in total control, *sin retains a foothold in our natures* because our physical bodies have not, as yet, been renewed. To use Puritan language again, there is such a thing as 'remaining sin'. Imagine a small, picturesque, historic city somewhere in England. Until six months ago everything in City Hall was a shambles. The chief executive was corrupt and lazy. Inefficiency was rife. Everyone, from heads of department down to low-grade clerks and even the tea lady, was out to get as much for themselves as they could. Alarmed by this state of affairs, the City Council insisted that a new chief executive be appointed. Now there is a new broom in charge, someone who means business! Every day a stream of directives goes out to all departments. The problem is that, even though City Hall is now under new management, many of the time-serving petty bureaucrats further down the chain of command are still in place. The new man meets obstruction, procrastination and delay right across the board. In the same way, the believer's life is under new management. A new man is in control and has set a new direction. Policy has changed at the highest level, but, lurking in the basement, certain elements loyal to the old management still cause as much trouble as they can. Just as the new boss at City Hall may have to weed out those members of the old guard who will not conform to the new direction, so the Christian must eradicate certain aspects of his old life. There is no place for sentiment.

2. Paul is not talking of self-mutilation

Thoughtful readers might also detect a second problem. On the face of it, a phrase like **'Put to death your members'** is worrying. What of countries like the Philippines where some Roman Catholics practise self-flagellation? Origen of Alexandria, one of the greatest theologians of the early church, took Jesus' statement that some 'have made themselves eunuchs for the kingdom of heaven's sake' (Matt. 19:12) literally and had himself castrated. Did Paul want his readers to amputate their limbs? In actual fact, Paul did not intend his readers to take the word **'members'** literally. It is an example of a figure of speech called metonymy, where our members, or limbs and organs, are used to represent the actions that we perform with them. (We use the same sort of figure in everyday speech when we say things like: 'Don't give me any of your lip,' or 'You are doing my head in!')

So, to sum up so far, 'Put to death your members' means that Christians must make every effort to exterminate sinful behaviour. There is a compelling reason why this matters so much. Paul's use of **'therefore'** connects this stark command with what has gone before in verses 1-4. Because we have been 'raised with Christ' (3:1), because we are no longer the people that we once were, since our life is 'hidden with Christ' (3:3) and it is our destiny to appear with Christ at his coming — for all these reasons the remaining sin in our lives must be stamped out.

Things that need killing (3:5)

We are now faced with a list of the things that need to be eradicated from every Christian's life. This list is not comprehensive. Sin is many-sided. If Paul had made an exhaustive list it would have been very large indeed. The believers in Colosse, however, could be sure that he had chosen to highlight matters that were very pertinent to their situation. Paul was addressing the fact that the pagan world of the Greek-speaking eastern Mediterranean was characterized by a sexual free-for-all. The collapse of the Christian consensus of a bygone era in many Western countries has left believers facing a similar situation. The area of sexual morality is one where Christians must stand out from the anarchy that prevails in society at large.

It is noticeable here that Paul proceeds from the outward to the inward, from the realm of our actions to the murky world of thoughts and impulses. To begin with, **'fornication'** translates the Greek *'porneia'*, from which our word 'pornography' is derived. It originally had the limited meaning of sex with prostitutes, but by Paul's day it had come to mean any kind of illicit sexual activity at all, any sexual liaison other than the union of one man and one woman in marriage.

'Uncleanness' is a rendering of the Greek *'akatharsia'*. It is the opposite of 'catharsis', the word that we use to describe an intense process of mental and emotional healing, where issues are resolved and hurts healed so that we are left 'clean'. Paul wanted his readers to understand that the opposite can happen. We can fill our minds with moral pollutants that leave us besmirched and dirty.

'Passion' and **'evil desire'** are related words. **'Passion'** describes what happens when our physical senses are swamped by the urge for fulfilment, and **'evil desire'** is the state of mind that takes us to that dangerous point. The best antidote is to distract our minds by filling them with thoughts of a very different character: 'Finally, brethren, whatever things are true, whatever things are noble, whatever things are just, whatever things are pure, whatever things are lovely, whatever things are of good report, if there is any virtue and if there is anything praiseworthy — meditate on these things' (Phil. 4:8).

Behind it all there is the sin of **'covetousness'**. Covetousness ranges far and wide. If we desire money or things, it can lead to theft. If we want prestige and status, it can lead us to use and exploit other people. If we are eaten up with longing for sexual gratification, it can lead to sexual sin. It is worth noting also that Paul saw covetousness as being tantamount to **'idolatry'**, as though the two sins were almost one and the same. An idol is a substitute for God and, at heart, the covetous person is a self-worshipper. He puts the satisfaction of his own appetites and longings where God ought to be. The best response is to seek contentment, to arrive at a settled conviction that my present circumstances, in every respect — including my present sex-life, or lack of one —

are what God wants for me at the present and that he knows best.

Why these things need killing (3:6-7)

Paul went on to give his friends in Colosse two incentives for being merciless in eradicating the remnants of sin from this present life.

1. These things merit God's judgement

First of all, it is **'because of these things'** that **'the wrath of God is coming upon the sons of disobedience'** (3:6). This verse needs to be read with care. It is not a suggestion that believers who fall into sexual sin might lose their salvation and become liable all over again to the judgement and the wrath of God. Praise the Lord, no true believer will ever have to fear the wrath of an offended God. Paul's thinking runs more along these lines: unbelievers will merit severe judgement, and rightly so. No believer would therefore want to live in a way that suggested that he actually belonged in the same category as those who deserve to be condemned. To look indistinguishable from people who have not been saved from sin, because we sin just as much and as obviously as they do, might even leave a hint of a miscarriage of justice in the air. At the end of all things, will anyone be left asking why we have been forgiven when our lifestyle is no different from that of people who were justly condemned?

2. These things belong to the old life

Secondly, Paul urged his readers to reflect on the fact that they too had **'once walked'** in these things (3:7). There are certain experiences in life where wisdom teaches us that

'Once bitten, twice shy.' Someone I know, in an idle moment at an Indian restaurant, touched the hotplate that was
there to keep his portion of Chicken Korma warm. He has
not, so far as I know, done the same thing again! Sin did us
no good the first time round, so why dabble with it now?

More drastic action required (3:8-9)

We now have a second list of the kind of things that need to
be eradicated by every follower of Jesus. Again, the list is
not exhaustive. Much more could have been said. This time
the list proceeds from the inward to the outward, from our
thought-life to our actual deeds. It would seem that in this
case Paul was concerned to promote good relationships
within the local church, since the sins in question largely
concern our attitudes to other people and the way that we
speak to them.

Why was this an issue in Colosse in particular? It probably arose because the teaching of the newcomers was
potentially divisive. When one element in a church lays
claim to experiences that others have not shared, insights
hidden from the majority and gifts that only seem to flourish
in their own circle, the favoured few can find it very tempting to boost themselves and disparage those without such
blessings. There is the temptation to cut themselves off from
ordinary believers because it is only possible to have real
fellowship with fellow initiates into the additional blessings
of those who have gone beyond the limited, ordinary Christianity preached by the likes of Epaphras and have been
admitted into 'fulness'.

It has to be said that the same kind of snobbery can be
found among other 'in-groups' in the evangelical world. Do
we ever give the impression that real fellowship is only

possible among those who know what we know, and think as we think — for example, those who read Reformed books?

There is a notable change of imagery at this point. In verse 5 Paul instructed his readers to put certain things to death. Now, in verse 8, they are told to **'put off'** certain things. This points ahead to verses 9-10, where the same expression is used. The central idea is that each Christian is a new person altogether. His old lifestyle is no longer appropriate, any more than it would be fitting for a person with a new, wholesome identity to go on wearing the clothes that he once wore in the days when he was, spiritually speaking, a corpse. Conversion to Christ does not involve a superficial or purely cosmetic change. It is as though the person that I used to be belongs firmly in the past. He has already been 'put off' (3:9) and a new identity, described here as 'the new man', has been 'put on' (3:10). Given that this is the case, the old man's wardrobe needs to be discarded too.

Paul begins with **'anger'** and **'wrath'** (3:8). There is considerable overlap between these two deeds that belong to the old nature. Perhaps he sees 'anger' as the seething cauldron within and 'wrath' as the outburst that flows from it. There is such a thing as righteous indignation, but I am always wary of those who use it as a justification for having a chronically short fuse. The Scriptures warn us that the human heart is perverse (Jer. 17:9) and that we should be suspicious of our motives. We should be doubly cautious before we give way to anger because it is often mixed with an element of self-serving: 'The wrath of man does not produce the righteousness of God' (James 1:20).

'Malice' describes the kind of vicious cruelty that uses words as weapons. **'Blasphemy'** translates the Greek *'blasphemia'*, a word with more than one meaning, depending on the context in which it is used. When it is used of speech against God, it does mean 'blasphemy' as we understand the word in English. In this case, however, it refers to malicious speech against others, especially within a local church. It would be best to render it 'slander'. In the same way, **'filthy language'** translates a Greek word that does not mean smutty talk so much as abusive talk. At this point, I have in mind two men. One of them has developed the delightful habit, whenever a third party is mentioned in his hearing, of saying something kind and affirming about that person. Someone else of my acquaintance is, sadly, quite different. When talking about other people, his stock in trade is bitter put-downs. It is no small matter to have acquired a reputation for being an 'accuser of the brethren' (Rev. 12:10). It says something about who we resemble.

Paul concludes this second list with a straight-from-the-shoulder charge: **'Do not lie to one another'** (3:9). At this point, Christians may need to be counter-cultural. In the East they may have to give up telling acceptable fictions to avoid 'losing face'. In the West they may need to stop masking the truth with expressions such as 'The cheque's in the post' or 'We must meet up some time.'

The old and the new (3:9-11)

This section closes with a vigorous restatement of the principle that Paul outlined at the beginning. Sinful behaviour, whether mentioned in Paul's two lists or not, is to be eradicated because Christians are what they are, people who have undergone a dramatic change. Here this change is pictured for us as a dramatic change of identity. Each believer has emphatically repudiated the person that he used to be; he has 'put off' that person, and so, along with **'the old man'**, he should also remove **'his deeds'** (3:9). The kind of behaviour that was typical of the person the Christian used to be but is no longer should be discarded as decisively as a man with a new suit puts his tattered old one out with the rubbish.

In the same way, since the believer has already acquired a new nature, having in effect put on **'the new man'**, he should also **'put on'** the appropriate qualities of character that go with this new identity. There are echoes here of Old Testament imagery and also of the fact that it was common in the first centuries of the Christian era for a newly baptized person to be given a clean white robe. The main point of the argument, however, is as clear as day. Those who have been given the breathtaking gift of a new life should live accordingly: 'How shall we who died to sin live any longer in it?' (Rom. 6:2).

The new man is not a static entity. Paul's description of the Christian as someone who is **'renewed in knowledge'** (3:10) would be better translated as someone who is *'being renewed in knowledge'*. This renewal is an ongoing process that begins at conversion, but which continues as the deeds appropriate to the old way of life are increasingly renounced and those appropriate to the new life are embraced. There are echoes here of Paul's teaching in Romans 12:2 that believers are to be transformed by the renewing of their minds. There is a definite goal in mind — namely, that believers should increasingly resemble their Creator; in other words, that the **'image'** of God, marred at the Fall, should become increasingly apparent in those who are Christ's new men and women.

Paul goes on to make a startling point, which again suggests that he had the unity of the church in Colosse very much in mind. New life, a new humanity, where each individual has as his goal the increasing recovery of the image of God, also involves new relationships. In Christ the old distinctions that divided people of different races and social backgrounds ought to disappear. 'Greeks' and 'Jews' (3:11) did not mix because of Israel's dietary laws. The Greeks regarded themselves as civilized people and, though they latterly awarded the Romans a certain grudging acceptance because they were too powerful to ignore, other nations were 'barbarians'.[2] The 'Scythians' were by common consent the most uncivilized people in the ancient world. Yet in Christ ethnic hatreds can be mastered. Can a **'slave'** ever have a natural relationship with a man who paid money for him? In Christ, Philemon and Onesimus can be brothers (see pages 215-34). In that case, is it too much for the members of one local church to get on with one another?

The section closes with the dramatic and triumphant declaration: **'But Christ is all and in all'** (3:11). The word **'but'** indicates a change of mood. Having listed a number of different categories into which the human race is divided, Paul notes that, for all the tragic reality of discord, while it is sadly true that humanity is split up into mutually hostile races, classes and sexes, **'Christ is all'**. He is all that matters and his greatness makes the divisions of mankind pale into insignificance. Furthermore, when he takes up residence in people of different kinds, when he is **'in all'**, the things that divide people are of far less weight than the great reality that unites them.

15.
A new set of clothes

Please read Colossians 3:12-17

The incentive to holy living (3:12)

In this section of his letter, the apostle Paul continues to plead with his readers to be what they are. Certain things are true of every Christian, whether living in the first or the twenty-first century. Each one has undergone a fundamental change, which affects his standing with God and his ultimate destiny. Having 'died with Christ' (2:20; 3:3), he is no longer the person he once was. That person is no more alive today than the dodo, the large flightless bird that once lived on the island of Mauritius. Instead, the Christian has been 'raised with Christ' (3:1) and is a new person altogether. His life, though still in a physical body, did not originate in this fallen world and does not belong to it. It is 'hidden with Christ in God' (3:3). And 'when Christ who is our life appears' (3:4), believers will appear with him, both as welcoming party and as escort for the coming King.

A Christian, then, is no ordinary person. He has a special status and his behaviour should reflect it. Speaking negatively, certain things must stop. We have already noted Paul's robust logic in verse 5: 'Therefore put to death your members which are on the earth...' Attitudes and behaviour that were typical of the life we once lived, and are still typical of society at large, must be comprehensively wiped out (3:6-7).

Now, in verse 12, we find a second **'therefore'**. Speaking positively, there are certain things that need to be done. The logic is equally forceful and insistent. Just as certain habits of thought and action are to be stamped out, it is every bit as pressing that the Christian should develop new habits to replace the old ones. While the 'old man' is to be 'put off' (3:9) as emphatically as a worn-out set of garments, the 'new man' is to be 'put on' (3:10) just as decisively and emphatically as a young man selected to play football for his country would, the first time he appeared in the national side, pull the jersey over his head that he had dreamed of wearing since boyhood and then square his shoulders. From verse 12 onwards, Paul explains what it means to adopt a distinctively Christian lifestyle, to put on the new man.

Paul begins by reminding his readers what Christians are. It is because certain things are true of us that a certain lifestyle is appropriate.

1. Christians have been chosen by God

First, Paul appealed to the church members in Colosse as **'the elect of God'**. No one ever became a Christian solely by his or her own choice. Behind our decision to follow Jesus lies the free choice of a sovereign God whose will can never be thwarted. It is a disturbing fact that some Christians react badly to this idea, as though there were something cold, arbitrary and manipulative about the way a merciful God exercises his royal prerogative to act as he sees fit. In any case, God chose us in Christ 'before the foundation of the world, that we should be holy and without blame before him in love' (Eph. 1:4). To be God's 'elect' is also to be his '**beloved**' (Paul's third phrase). To be chosen by God and to be loved by God are one and the same thing.

2. Christians are set apart for God

In second place, we are told that Christians are '**holy**', set apart for the service of God. This is the very reason why God chose them, to 'be holy and without blame before him'.

3. Christians are God's special treasure

These words, addressed to first-century Christians living in a town in Asia Minor that had seen better days, are strongly reminiscent of words spoken through Moses to the people of ancient Israel: 'For you are a holy people to the LORD your God; the LORD your God has chosen you to be a people for himself, a special treasure above all the peoples on the face of the earth. The LORD did not set his love on you nor choose you because you were more in number than any other people, for you were the least of all peoples; but because the LORD loves you, and because he would keep the oath which he swore to your fathers, the LORD has brought you out with a mighty hand, and redeemed you from the house of bondage, from the hand of Pharaoh king of Egypt...' (Deut. 7:6-8). What was once true of Israel as a nation was now equally true of a modest gathering of Christians.

It is also true of every gathering of Christian people. We may not amount to much, but God looks upon us as elect, holy and his particular treasure. The believers in Colosse needed to be reminded of that. The new teachers who had made a takeover bid for the church encouraged a kind of spiritual elitism, hinting that the ordinary church, with its ordinary believers, was not at the cutting edge. Those who wished to be part of God's new thing should look elsewhere for their fellowship. Paul's argument, however, is that every

Christian, no matter how modest and nondescript he might be in his own eyes, or in the eyes of those who think themselves more spiritual, is called to spiritual excellence because, in spite of appearances, he is part of God's Israel, a royal priesthood. Chosen by God, holy in his sight and the object of his special love — is that not enough of an incentive to 'put on the new man'? (3:10).

Five new garments (3:12-13)

What follows is a list of five moral qualities. The Christian is to 'put them on', to embellish his life with them, as deliberately and consciously as someone getting dressed for a special occasion selects his clothing, or a lady might choose her outfit for her daughter's wedding.

.

1. A heart of compassion

The first quality is **'tender mercies'**. The AV's phrase, 'bowels of mercies', is an accurate, if slightly earthy, rendering of the Greek. The ancients thought that the stomach and intestines were the seat of the emotions, much like the way that we today speak of the heart. Paul's words therefore had the same force as 'a heart of mercy', or 'a heart of compassion'. What Paul envisages is not a superficial emotion, but something that comes from deep inside. To be like that is to be like God himself, who is 'the Father of mercies and God of all comfort' (2 Cor. 1:3). We can see this quality at work in the life of Joseph, firstly in his reaction upon seeing his brother Benjamin for the first time in many years (Gen. 43:30), and secondly upon being reunited with all of his brothers (Gen. 45:1-14).

2. Kindness

The second item is **'kindness'**, the opposite of the 'malice' described in verse 8. Again, this is a quality that belongs to God himself. The opening line of Psalm 34:8 can be rendered: 'Oh, taste and see that the LORD is kind...' It is the kindness of the Lord that leads us to repentance (Rom. 2:4). Through the gospel, 'The kindness and the love of God our Saviour toward man appeared' (Titus 3:4). We see examples of this kindness at work in human hearts in the case of the Good Samaritan in Jesus' parable (Luke 10:25-37) and in the life of Barnabas (Acts 4:36-37). There is ample evidence that Paul too was a kind man. One example occurs in 1 Thessalonians 2:9, where we read of his reluctance to be a burden on the believers in Thessalonica.

3. Humility

In third place we meet **'humility'**. The Colossian believers had only recently emerged from a background steeped in paganism. To most pagans humility was not a virtue but a weakness. The humble man had no sense of his own worth. His honour meant nothing to him. A crucified Saviour will always be puzzling, even offensive, to people with a highly developed sense of honour. How could one who was truly God accept such humiliation? And yet, humility is the will of God for all his people:

> He has shown you, O man, what is good;
> And what does the LORD require of you
> But to do justly,
> To love mercy,
> And to walk humbly with your God?

(Micah 6:8).

Paul's argument that the believers in Philippi should embrace humility is tied in very closely with the fact that we have a humble Saviour. His tender plea, 'Let nothing be done through selfish ambition or conceit, but in lowliness of mind let each esteem others better than himself,' is amplified later on: 'Let this mind be in you which was also in Christ Jesus.' And Jesus is the one who, in his incarnation, 'made himself of no reputation' (Phil. 2:3,5,7). As Martin Luther graphically put it, he made himself nothing. The biggest 'somebody' in the universe made himself a nobody. The apostle Peter's charge, 'Be clothed with humility' (1 Peter 5:5), reminds us of one who wrapped himself in a towel and washed his disciples' feet.

4. Meekness

'Meekness', in fourth place, was supremely the virtue of Moses, who did not give way to rage when he met all kinds of unfair obstruction (Num. 12:3). It is one aspect of the 'fruit of the Spirit' (Gal. 5:23, where it is translated as 'gentleness'). Given that this quality only occurs where God the Holy Spirit is at work in a human personality, it clearly does not come naturally. The normal human reaction to provocation is prickly self-assertion. It is particularly challenging to observe where this quality is considered most appropriate. Restoring a sinning brother is work for those with a 'spirit of meekness' (Gal. 6:1, AV), not for those who ooze moral superiority. It is also a requirement for those defending the faith: 'A servant of the Lord must not quarrel but be gentle to all, able to teach, patient, in humility correcting those who are in opposition, if God perhaps will grant them repentance...' (2 Tim. 2:24-25). 'Always be ready to give a defence to everyone who asks you a reason for the hope that is in you, with meekness and fear' (1 Peter 3:15). Calvinists of the spiky variety take note!

5. Patience

Our list concludes with **'long-suffering'**, or patience. If God were not patient no one would ever be saved: 'The long-suffering of our Lord is salvation' (2 Peter 3:15). This quality is explained in more detail in verse 13. When Paul wrote of **'bearing with one another'**, did his thoughts go back to the church in Corinth, where members took one another to court? 'Why do you not rather accept wrong? Why do you not rather let yourselves be cheated?' (1 Cor. 6:7). Christians still need to learn patience. The habit of saying, 'That person is impossible!' did not die out with Euodia and Syntyche (Phil. 4:2). In the same way, to with-hold forgiveness when Christ has forgiven each one of us so much is mean-spirited.

Before we leave this list behind, let us note two points in passing. Firstly, every one of the qualities that Paul mentions is to do with relationships. A local church where these are in evidence will be a happy community. Was Paul trying to correct some of the damage done by the newcomers, whose 'super-spirituality' tended to create churches made up of superiors and inferiors, the inner circle and the excluded? Secondly, it is also worth noting that putting on these qualities will make us resemble God himself. That should be incentive enough.

A new coat (3:14)

In addition to the qualities already noted, the Christian must **'put on love'**. And this item from the spiritual wardrobe must be put on **'above all these things'**. The other qualities matter very much. This matters even more. The 'fruit of the Spirit' mentioned in Galatians 5:22-23 is like a cluster of grapes. Nine individual fruits hang together in the one cluster. Love is mentioned first. It is the one Christian grace that is absolutely indispensable: 'Though I speak with the tongues of men and of angels, but have not love, I have become sounding brass or a clanging cymbal. And though I have the gift of prophecy, and understand all mysteries and all knowledge, and though I have all faith, so that I could remove mountains, but have not love, I am nothing. And though I bestow all my goods to feed the poor, and though I give my body to be burned, but have not love, it profits me nothing' (1 Cor. 13:1-3).

In a local community of Christians, love is the **'bond of perfection'**, perhaps better translated as the 'bond of unity'. It fastens a church together. We read in Acts 27:17 that Paul was once on board a ship that threatened to break up. Ropes were passed right round the hull to prevent the timbers from coming apart. Whatever else we lack, may the Lord teach us to love one another in a truly biblical way.

Pay attention to the umpire (3:15)

Paul went on to challenge his readers to **'let the peace of God rule'** in their hearts. In secular Greek, the word translated **'peace'** (*eirene*) was sometimes used to describe a formal treaty that brought an end to hostilities between two warring cities. 'A peace' had been concluded. It was also used to describe the state of calm and well-being that followed the official conclusion of peace and flowed from it. Here Paul has something similar in mind.

Some people are peaceable by nature. They have an equable temperament and are not easily upset. By contrast, Paul is speaking of a peace that is supernatural in origin. The **'peace of God'** means more than just ordinary tranquillity. Inward peace of heart and mind is only possible because of all that God has done in Christ to be reconciled to those who were once his enemies. When someone becomes a Christian he lays down his arms and takes no further part in the long war that mankind has waged against God. And this cessation of hostilities leads in turn to a flourishing state of soul. The 'peace of God' garrisons the heart and mind against threats from outside (Phil. 4:7). It is clearly supernatural. People looking on are often amazed at the calm serenity of the Christian in situations that would leave other people frantic. It 'surpasses all understanding'.

Here, in Colossians 3:15, believers are encouraged to 'let the peace of God rule' in their hearts. The word translated **'rule'** describes the action of an umpire. Some fine believers make the mistake at this point of concluding that this verse is about decision-making on the part of individual Christians. Suppose we are faced by two options: we are in turmoil about the one, but have a sense of peace about the other. Seen in this way, the 'umpire' is the sense of calm within a believer that prompts him to choose the course of action that will leave him relaxed and unruffled. In response to this, we must remember that the human heart is deceitful (Jer. 17:9). It plays tricks on us. Our innate capacity to be self-serving may well make us nervous of doing the right thing but easy in our minds about something dubious.

In any case, Paul's description of the 'peace of God' acting like an umpire is not so much to do with peace in the heart of one person, who would otherwise be at odds with himself, but peace instead of tension and strife between believers in a given local church. In other words, God's gift of 'peace' has a crucial role in keeping churches together. The fact that a church is at peace should be a strong incentive to do nothing that would threaten this precious tranquillity. The new teachers in Colosse threatened the peace of the church by creating an atmosphere where the spiritually elevated wrote off everyone else. In one church that I knew a particular group never came to the prayer meeting. They couldn't, they said, get real fellowship there. Instead they organized a meeting of their own to which only the select few who shared their insights were invited. Christians are called to live **'in one body'**. It is no small matter to keep a church together. It is telling that thankfulness is mentioned in the same connection. If we can keep at the forefront of our joint lives a shared sense of amazement at what God has done for us in Christ, we will be less likely to fall out.

Pay attention to the 'word of Christ' (3:16)

Paul's next challenge, **'Let the word of Christ dwell in you richly'**, was intended as a corrective to one damaging aspect of the situation in Colosse. There had been no shortage of words there in the recent past, particularly of authoritative pronouncements from the new teachers, but Jesus is the only Lord and teacher of the church. His words not only take precedence over all others; they exclude all others. Every other teacher only deserves a hearing in so far as he reflects the word of Christ with scrupulous accuracy.

The phrase **'dwell in you richly'** invites us to become soaked, saturated and marinated in the word of Christ from the inside out. (Spurgeon said of John Bunyan that his blood was 'Bibline'. If you pricked him, he would bleed Bible verses.) A Christian community will not be happy if the word of Christ is not abundantly available so that the people of God can read, study, hear and live it out. Incidentally, this goes hand in hand with Paul's plea to the Christians in Ephesus, and believers in every generation since, to 'be filled with the Spirit' (Eph. 5:18). Since God the Holy Spirit wrote the Bible, we cannot walk in step with him if we ignore what he has written. Ultimately a church which neglects the Word of God silences the Spirit of God.

Two practical consequences follow on from this. (The punctuation of verse 16 is actually very difficult.)

1. The central role of teaching

Firstly, a church must give pride of place to **'teaching and admonishing** [or instructing] **one another'**. Whatever else gets squeezed out, this must not. It is a sad commentary on contemporary Christianity that in many circles there has been a steady erosion of the place given to the public teaching of the Word of God. We should just note in passing that Paul's phrase, **'one another'**, suggests that this teaching should not be the exclusive preserve of a single person, but equally the fact that it is to be done **'in all wisdom'** (this phrase should follow on from the words 'one another') suggests a need for maturity on the part of those who teach it.

2. The effect on our singing

Secondly, Paul's logic is that if the word of Christ is at home in our hearts, this will affect our singing. **'Psalms and hymns and spiritual songs'**, by the way, are not exact synonyms, although there is probably some overlap. The word **'psalms'** points us back to the Old Testament, to the book of praises inspired by the Holy Spirit. According to Augustine, a 'hymn' will have three elements. It must be sung; it must strike the note of praise; and it must be directed to God. Understood in this way, many of the psalms are also hymns. Nevertheless, there are hymns in Scripture outside the Old Testament Psalter, notably Mary's song, also known as the Magnificat (Luke 1:46-55) and the song of Zacharias called the Benedictus (Luke 1:68-79). Most Christians would also accept that devotional poems intended to be sung to God, which are an accurate expression of scriptural truth even though the exact words may not be found in the Bible, may be classed as hymns and sung with profit. A 'spiritual song' would be a song with a spiritual and edifying theme, but which may not take the form of direct praise to God.

What we choose to sing speaks volumes about our spiritual experience. Your favourite hymn will say something about what you are as a Christian. Paul's case here is that our first concern should be to sing truth. Since we are singing **'to the Lord'**, anything else would dishonour him. The church in every age therefore needs to ensure that it is careful about what it sings. Do we sing Scripture itself? Are the other things that we sing entirely agreeable to what Scripture says? I have no quarrel with modern hymns as such and have come to love many of them. It also needs to be said that the mere fact that a hymn or song has been around for some decades is no guarantee of its quality. A hymn, whether old or new, stands or falls entirely by what it says. But it is worth noting that, while our praise is primarily directed towards God, it is also directed towards each other. Good hymns teach truth and depth of experience.[1] Do we sing about God, or our own feelings? What are we learning from what we sing?

It is also important that we sing in the right frame of mind and heart. Paul encouraged the believers in Colosse to sing **'with grace'** in their hearts. The ESV is probably correct in rendering the original here as 'with thankfulness'.[2] Our singing will be perfunctory and mechanical unless it stems from a sense of warm gratitude for all that God has done for us in Christ. Surely Christians have a song in their hearts because they are filled with amazement at the grace of God. Knowing how much they owe, their appreciation shows itself in song.

Conclusion: an all-embracing command (3:17)

Our section closes with a general exhortation that is universal in scope. Every aspect of the believer's life is covered: **'Whatever you do in word or deed, do all in the name of the Lord Jesus, giving thanks to God the Father through him.'** We have already seen that Christianity is not a hobby. In this chapter the apostle has encouraged us to 'put on' certain qualities, to live together in love and peace and let the word of Christ control what is taught and sung among us. Now in conclusion we have a clear call to bring our every moment and every action under the lordship of Christ.

In recent months there has been a steady stream of white Britons turning to Islam. One of the reasons that such converts often give is that their new religion offers not just a set of opinions, but an all-embracing lifestyle suitable for people with an all-or-nothing temperament. On reflection this can only mean that contemporary Christianity has fallen far short of what Paul envisages here. For the wholehearted believer no part of life is to be exempt from the claims of Jesus.

16.
The Christian home

Please read Colossians 3:18-21

We have been considering what it means to live a distinctly Christian lifestyle, or what it involves in practice, now that the 'old man', the person that the Christian used to be, is no more, to 'put off' the kind of deeds that were habitual to him (3:9). By contrast, since the Christian is a new person altogether, he is to 'put on' the kind of deeds that are appropriate to his new identity (3:10). The Christian life is not lived in isolation. All the moral qualities that the Christian is to 'put on' concern the way that we relate to other people. The focus in verses 12-17 has been on relationships within the local church. By contrast, from verse 18 onwards, the focus shifts to a new set of relationships, those within the Christian home.

Like the parallel passage in Ephesians 5:18 – 6:9, three sets of relationships are in view: husbands and wives; parents and children; masters and servants. Martin Luther referred to this section as the 'House Table', a table of responsibilities and duties for the Christian family. In this chapter we shall consider the first two pairs — husbands and wives, and parents and children. The third pairing, masters and servants, deserves separate treatment, partly because circumstances in the developed world today are very different from those in

Paul's day. Then it was not unusual for the master-servant relationship to exist within the household of a reasonably prosperous family. In the West today, however, the nearest equivalent relationship is the one that exists in the work-place. Our theme, then, in the present chapter is the Christian home.

A raw deal?

Many modern readers find Paul's words about submission, particularly that of women, to be highly objectionable. It is assumed that submission has built into it the ideas of su-periority and inferiority and that it is no basis for a worth-while relationship. If someone insists that he is better than I am, our friendship will never be on a mature footing. One party will be condescending and supercilious; the other will pretend a fawning obsequiousness while burning with resentment. Some people come to Paul's words with their minds made up, as though he was advocating a 'toadies' charter' where husbands and fathers get the best of a very one-sided deal, while wives and children, on the other hand, are firmly put in their place.

1. Submission as a principle that applies to all Christians

In response to such thinking, it is important that we grasp the fact that submission is not simply the lot of females and minors, condemned to a life of oppression by virtue of the fact that men are physically stronger, but is an essential part of what it is to be a Christian. There are certain contexts in which all Christians must acknowledge the rightful claims of a higher authority.

Our most important relationship, the one that we enjoy with God himself, is not one of equals. We relate to God as inferiors; he, by contrast, has no equals. As created beings we worship our Creator. We stand before the Judge of all the earth as plaintiffs. He is the lawmaker; we are lawbreakers. He is the Emperor of the whole vast universe; we are subjects. As the sovereign Lord of all things, he is the master and we are only servants. At every level of our being he has a right to claim our allegiance and exact our obedience. In the same way, the fact that we call Jesus Christ 'Lord' means that we admit that he is entitled to homage, respect, loyal service and unfailing obedience. Jesus' question, 'But why do you call me "Lord, Lord," and do not do the things which I say?' (Luke 6:46), only makes sense on the assumption that as Lord he has the right to demand obedience from his followers.

But submission does not stop there. Writing to the believers in Rome, Paul insisted that 'every soul' should be 'subject to the governing authorities' (Rom. 13:1), since the latter derive their authority from God himself. Paul's phrase, 'every soul', forbids us the luxury of supposing that we are exempt if we do not like the government that we have. The apostle Peter uses very similar language: 'Submit yourselves to every ordinance of man for the Lord's sake, whether to the king as supreme, or to governors, as to those who are sent by him for the punishment of evildoers and for the praise of those who do good. For this is the will of God ...' (1 Peter 2:13-15). When the command was given to 'Fear God,' and 'Honour the king' (1 Peter 2:17), the king in question was Nero.

In the same way, the under-shepherds, who rule over the scattered flocks of the Great Shepherd himself, have a right to expect compliance and loyalty from the sheep that they serve (Heb. 13:7), even though their rule is to be as gentle as that of a nursing mother (1 Thess. 2:7).

Perhaps the most telling injunction anywhere in Paul's writings, however, is found in Ephesians 5:21. Spirit-filled people are called to submit 'to one another in the fear of God'. Not all can assert the claims proper to authority, but love has its claims too, and for love's sake each must submit to all, and all to each. Within a local church, older friends might sometimes yield to the younger; the elders might choose not to force an issue; a majority might yield to a minority; and the men might add their names to the catering and cleaning rotas. It is a gross caricature to suggest that Paul envisaged men lording it over women, while children should be seen and not heard. Every Christian male should echo the words of a soldier who knew both his rank and his place: 'I … am a man placed under authority' (Luke 7:8).

2. A distinctively Christian form of submission

There is another dimension to this matter of submission. Lists of domestic duties and responsibilities were not unusual in the ancient world. Several such lists have survived. This list, however, is not merely a summary of desirable qualities. It is distinctively Christian. Wives are to submit to their husbands 'as is fitting in the Lord' (3:18). Children are to be obedient because 'this is well pleasing to the Lord' (3:20).

Why is submission 'fitting', an appropriate virtue for a follower of Jesus? Those who bridle at the idea of sub-mission often quote Paul's words in Galatians 3:28: 'There is neither Jew nor Greek, there is neither slave nor free, there is neither male nor female; for you are all one in Christ Jesus.' If a Christian woman is the equal of her husband, both as a human being and as a Christian, how can she be subject to him?

3. The example of Jesus

It is critically important at this point that we consider Jesus. His enemies criticized him because he made 'himself equal

with God' (John 5:18). He was no less divine than his Father
was. All that can be said of the Father's Godhead can be said
in equal measure of the Son's. Nevertheless, the Son is
subject to the Father. Speaking of his Father, Jesus said, 'I
always do those things that please him' (John 8:29). Whenever, as Christians, we are called upon to place ourselves
under the authority of another, our model is the one who
took 'the form of a bondservant ... [and] humbled himself'
(Phil. 2:7,8). Our pattern for subjection is Jesus himself.
Even on the night he was betrayed, Jesus' disciples insisted
on asserting their places in the pecking order. 'When he had
washed their feet, taken his garments, and sat down again, he
said to them, "Do you know what I have done to you? You
call me Teacher and Lord, and you say well, for so I am. If I
then, your Lord and Teacher, have washed your feet, you
also ought to wash one another's feet. For I have given you
an example, that you should do as I have done to you"'
(John 13:12-15). Faced with that kind of logic, can any
believer justifiably say, 'Why should I lower myself?' Look
who lowered himself!

The duty of wives (3:18)

Wives are to submit to their husbands, to place themselves
under their authority. On the one hand, this is to be a voluntary act. There is to be no coercion. A Christian lady is to do
so willingly, with her eyes wide open. On the other hand,
Christian ladies in general are not required to submit to men
in general, but only to their own husbands. (Some evangelical males see the whole feminine sex as a gigantic pool of
potential menials.) It is sometimes argued that, in saying this,
Paul was merely reflecting the culture of his day, as though
you would expect a first-century Jewish rabbi to say that sort
of thing, but times have changed. Strangely enough, those

who make this sort of case do not go on to argue that modern men can stop loving their wives for the same reason! In fact I suspect that wifely submission has always gone against the grain. It was tough in the first century; it is still tough now. It involves self-denial, the very thing that all Christians are called to. And this is by no means Paul's only utterance on the subject: 'I want you to know that the head of every man is Christ, the head of woman is man, and the head of Christ is God' (1 Cor. 11:3). Mature women are 'to be discreet, chaste, homemakers, good, obedient to their own husbands, that the word of God may not be blasphemed' (Titus 2:5). (This ought to be balanced against the fact that the virtuous woman in Proverbs 31 whose price is 'above rubies' also ran a thriving business.)

At the same time, submission is not absolute. No husband has a right to insist that his wife do something that God forbids. The Puritan author William Gouge expressed this rather quaintly: 'If an husband shall command his wife to go to Mass, to a stage play, to play at dice, to prostitute her body to uncleanness, to go garishly and whorishly attired, to sell by scant weights, short measures or the like, she ought not to do so.'[1] To put it in more modern terms, no Christian man should persuade his wife to say that it was she who drove the car much too fast past the speed camera on the nearby stretch of motorway because he already has several penalty points on his driving licence. For the same reason, he must not trample on her conscience.

Nevertheless, submission is a biblical requirement. For the married Christian lady, submission to the Lord requires no less than submission to her husband. This does, however, invite some reflection. Do most men realize just how much they ask of a woman when they propose marriage? It is no small matter to request that a spirited and capable person give up her independence, as one who is answerable directly to God, and submit herself to the headship of another. A lot of men give much thought to the qualities of the ideal woman, someone who will meet all their needs and satisfy all their requirements. But how many men reflect on their own qualities, asking whether they are the kind of man that a good woman would willingly and gladly submit to? I have known some fine Christian girls who have regretfully concluded that the believing men of their acquaintance are too weak and inconsistent to merit that kind of cheerful submission.

The duty of husbands (3:19)

Husbands are commanded, first of all, to love their wives. It might seem strange to some modern people that Paul commands his male readers to love. Jesus, of course, did the same with his 'new commandment' that Christians love one another (John 13:34). But surely you cannot command people to love, any more than you can say, 'Happy Christmas — and that's an order!'? We think that way because we are conditioned to regard love as a word that mainly has to do with our feelings. Thus, 'I don't love you any more,' means, 'I no longer have the feelings for you that I once did.' In point of fact, feelings often follow actions. When we deliberately and consciously set ourselves to act well towards someone, a new regard may spring up in our affections.

The parallel passage in Ephesians 5 leaves us in no doubt that husbands are required to love their wives to an extraordinary degree, 'as Christ also loved the church and gave himself for her' (Eph. 5:25). Few godly women would mind submitting to men who could love like that, and that kind of husband would not insist on an exaggerated or demeaning subjection. The head of a family will not subject the heart of that same family to petty subjugation. I have observed the way that some Muslim ladies in the East walk demurely two paces behind their husbands. I can't understand it. I always supposed that a proposal of marriage was tantamount to saying, 'Please walk by my side through the wilderness of this world.'

The positive command to love is reinforced by a negative command. There is no place for bitterness in the way a Christian husband treats his wife, as though she has become a disappointment to him. One American commentator charges husbands not to call their wives 'honey' while acting like vinegar. And if sourness and disillusionment are not to take hold, as Paul says elsewhere, 'he who is married' should make it his business to seek 'how he may please his wife' (1 Cor. 7:33).

The duty of children (3:20)

The Greek word translated **'children'** does not refer to a specific age-group, such as very small children, but to all who are still living under the parental roof and who are therefore under their parents' authority. This is a theme that we meet often in Scripture. In Ephesians 6:2-3, Paul makes a direct appeal to the Ten Commandments: ' "Honour your father and mother," which is the first commandment with promise: "that it may be well with you and you may live long on the earth" ' (cf. Exod. 20:12).

The book of Proverbs contains a number of poignant descriptions of the fall-out that occurs when children do not heed this warning: 'A wise son makes a glad father, but a foolish son is the grief of his mother' (Prov. 10:1). Parents make an enormous emotional investment in their children. It is a particularly cruel disillusionment when lives that once promised much are wasted: 'A foolish son is a grief to his father, and bitterness to her who bore him' (Prov. 17:25).

Furthermore, the grief and regrets are one-sided: 'A foolish man despises his mother' (Prov. 15:20).

We should also note that unruly and unmanageable children are one of the marks of a collapsing culture and a society under judgement (Rom. 1:30). Paul warned Timothy that a rebellious youth culture will mark human civilization in 'the last days', by which he meant the period of history inaugurated at the first coming of Christ and which will be with us until he returns. 'But know this, that in the last days perilous times will come: for men will be lovers of themselves, lovers of money, boasters, proud, blasphemers, disobedient to parents...' (2 Tim. 3:1).

Timothy was instructed to 'turn away' from people like that (2 Tim. 3:5). Christian young people who follow his example may have to go against the prevailing culture and in so doing leave their contemporaries in no doubt that the gospel changes things. Many an inexperienced young Christian asks, 'What is the will of God for my life?' A good place to start is to make sure that your relationship with your parents is on a godly footing. Do people in your peer group speak of their parents as though they were the opposition, there to be hoodwinked, milked for cash and otherwise ignored? Do you have brothers or sisters? Would you like them to become Christians too? All your efforts will be undermined if, day in, day out, they see you being disobliging and belligerent to the parents you have in common.

The duties of fathers (3:21)

It is interesting that Paul mentions **'fathers'** here, rather than parents, presumably because of their role as heads of families. Fathers, for their part, are charged not to **'provoke'** their children, not to exasperate them, in case they become disheartened. It is a bitter legacy to leave behind if, when our children think of us, the phrases that spring to mind are things like: 'He's always finding fault,' or 'Nothing I do ever satisfies him.'

There are many unfolding tragedies in the United Kingdom today. One of the worst is the prevalence of fathers who are either absent or who are present but have opted out of real fatherhood. Presumably the gangs of teenagers who go on drunken rampages after closing time on Saturday nights have biological fathers. But where are they? Every girl who becomes a lap dancer, poses for pornographic magazines or descends into the shady world of the streetwalker would never have been born at all but for a father playing his part at the time of conception. But this is what makes fatherhood a particularly difficult art. In contemporary society children are growing up without consistent discipline. They are left to discover that there are few real boundaries.

Paul's warning here is that fathers can overbalance and err on the other side of child-rearing by breaking a young person's spirit. This can be done by being overprotective and stifling opportunities to learn independence, by unrelenting criticism and stinted praise, by letting a child know that he or she has fallen short of expectations that were never realistic in the first place, and by making pointed comparisons either with siblings or with children from another family, who are presented as if they were perfect. (The only thing that this will achieve is to make your children develop a cordial dislike for the ones they are compared with.) Very few fathers who read Paul's words will not feel rueful at some point and be grateful that both God and our children are forgiving.

Conclusion

There is something slippery about the human heart. In particular, faced with a table of family duties like this one, we can find it all too easy to impose conditions. A wife says to herself, 'I will submit to him, but only when he starts to show me some sacrificial love.' Is it possible that her husband is taking the same line? 'I would love her in the way that I ought, but not till she shows a bit of respect.' Children can play the same game: 'Obey them? Dream on, not unless they show me a bit of affection!' In the meantime, resentful parents are thinking, 'Why should I be affectionate when the only return I get is surly non-cooperation?' The problem here is that each person is looking at the other party rather than himself or herself. We would do well at such moments to remember Jesus' words to Peter: 'What is that to you? You follow me' (John 21:22).

17.
The Christian in the workplace

Please read Colossians 3:22 – 4:1

These verses continue the section which begins at 3:18, the table of responsibilities and duties for the Christian family. We have already considered what the apostle Paul had to say about two pairs of relationships, those between husbands and wives and between parents and children. We now come to a third pair of relationships. How should 'masters' and 'bond-servants', or slaves, treat one another? It was natural for Paul to group all of these relationships together (cf. Eph. 5:22 – 6:9) since, at that time, many families would have included a number of slaves. Even a modest household might include one or two, who would work alongside the master and mistress. A wealthy family would have a great many slaves, who would free their owners for a life of luxury.

The institution of slavery was very pervasive in the ancient world. One estimate has it that one third of the population of Rome was made up of slaves. Some were prisoners of war; some were criminals sentenced to a life of slavery by the courts; some were purchased from lands outside the empire; and others were the children of slave parents. It is highly likely that some of the believers in Colosse were slaves and others, probably fewer in number, would be slave-owners. (Perhaps this is why Paul gives more space to the duties of slaves than to those of their masters.)

There is no doubt that these verses pose a real problem for many modern readers. It is now universally agreed that slavery is a great moral evil. The city of Lancaster, where I have served as a minister of the gospel for almost two decades, is one of several cities in the United Kingdom tainted by association with the 'triangular trade'[1] which saw hundreds of thousands of Africans transported to what were then the British colonies in North America. Some of the most attractive buildings in Lancaster once served a thriving trade based on the capture and exploitation of human beings. While slavery still exists, it is no longer out in the open. Those who practise it try to keep it hidden. It is only when incidents occur like the tragic deaths of Chinese cockle-pickers in Morecambe Bay in the north-west of England, who were cruelly exploited by ruthless gang-masters, that people in Western nations, with their comfortable existence, are reminded that something very like slavery does still exist in our world.

An overview of the Bible's attitude to slavery

It is clear that, as far as Paul was concerned, in spiritual terms at least, the old inequality had been abolished. In Christ there is 'neither slave nor free' (Gal. 3:28). But in that case, why did Paul not simply condemn slavery outright? If masters and slaves were on the same footing as Christians, why should they not be on the same footing in law? It is a terrible blot on the history of the Christian church that some believers have complacently justified the practices of owning and buying slaves. Even so, Christians who thought like that did not have the Bible on their side and it is not fair to Paul to assume that he was lukewarm on the issue.

1. The Old Testament background

Note, first of all, that the laws that made up the national covenant between Israel and God include a robust condemnation of overpowering people and selling them as slaves: 'He who kidnaps a man and sells him, or if he is found in his hand, shall surely be put to death' (Exod. 21:16). Had Joseph's brothers been alive after the law was given at Sinai, their treatment of Joseph would have incurred the death penalty.

Slavery as it was practised throughout the Roman Empire was virtually unknown in ancient Israel. A powerful racial memory meant that the Jews could not think of it without a shudder. When the national covenant was ratified in the plains of Moab, God could appeal for decent treatment for resident foreigners in Israel with words such as these: 'You shall remember that you were a slave in the land of Egypt...' (Deut. 15:15). A further period of exile in Babylon helped to reinforce this collective sense of abhorrence.

An Israelite who fell into serious debt could sell himself into indentured servitude, but stringent restrictions were in force to ensure that this never became permanent. There was a maximum term of seven years. Once this was over, the master was required to provide the former servant with enough capital to start out on his own again.

A system of forced labour was sometimes imposed on foreign prisoners of war, and in Joshua's day an ethnic minority known as the Gibeonites had been enslaved in commutation of the death penalty, but in general slavery was only practised in Israel during times of marked national spiritual and moral decline.

The prophets were unsparing in their condemnation of it: 'This is the word that came to Jeremiah from the LORD, after King Zedekiah had made a covenant with all the people who were at Jerusalem to proclaim liberty to them: that every man should set free his male and female slave — a Hebrew man or woman — that no one should keep a Jewish brother in bondage' (Jer. 34:8-9).

2. The New Testament view

With this kind of background, it is not surprising that Paul wrote as he did in 1 Timothy 1:9-10, where capturing and enslaving people is listed alongside several other grievous sins: 'The law is not made for a righteous person, but for the lawless and insubordinate, for the ungodly and for sinners, for the unholy and profane, for murderers of fathers and murderers of mothers, for manslayers, for fornicators, for sodomites, for kidnappers, for liars, for perjurers.' We have no reason at all to suppose that Paul in particular approved of slavery, and good reason in general to suppose that the Bible condemns it.

If we are to be fair to Paul, we should also note that it was completely impractical for first-century Christians, a tiny minority within a sprawling empire and with no access to the levers of power, to work for the abolition of an institution that underpinned the whole economic system of the time. It was difficult enough for William Wilberforce and his friends, several of them members of Parliament, to stir the conscience of a nation with an accountable system of government. Nineteenth-century Britain was not yet a full-blown democracy, but it was certainly not the absolute monarchy that Rome was.

Paul's aim was both more limited and more radical. If the wholesale abolition of slavery was not yet a viable proposition, the transformation of individual relationships was. Lives are changed by the power of the gospel. It follows that even an oppressive relationship based on exploitation can be altered for the better. This is why Paul's words are still relevant in a very different setting. Relationships in a modern workplace can be very fraught, with both management and labour trying to use and outwit the other. Paul's challenge is that, whichever side of the divide we find ourselves on, we learn to think of our role in a new way. Let the slave concentrate on his freedom and the master on his servitude.

The Christian slave is free from fear (3:22)

Paul instructed Christian slaves to obey their human masters **'in all things'**. On the one hand, this means that first-century slaves and twenty-first century employees should not only comply with instructions that are easy and pleasant, but also with those that are tedious or disagreeable. On the other hand, 'all things' does not include those things that are displeasing to God. As with every other clash of loyalties, Christian slaves in the first century sometimes had to suffer because they put Jesus first. Should modern believers be any different? Nevertheless, Paul set out to address the main failing of the whole system of slave labour. Force someone to work against his will, and he will begrudge every drop of sweat and resent every second of toil. Slaves then and reluctant employees now will try to undermine a system that grinds them down.

One response is to act a part, working **'with eye-service, as men-pleasers'**. This mentality is summed up in the phrase: 'When the boss is looking, look busy'; in other words, do the absolute minimum but don't let it show. In a slave economy, sullenness, shoddy work and spiteful acts of sabotage were common. And today, in most factories, offices, schools and colleges, or anywhere where there is a sizeable workforce, there are pockets of devious types who see the management as an enemy to be outwitted at all costs by way of slacking, pilfering, clock-watching, moonlighting and obstructionism. In some workplaces the habit is so ingrained that it is assumed that everyone is underhand. (I remember one schoolteacher who always came into the staffroom at a run with a file under his arm, puffing and blowing. He would scan the board where notices were displayed, wipe his forehead and, with a loud 'Phew!', dash straight out again. He was actually a conscientious man but those in cynics' corner wore a smirk that said, 'We know what you're up to!') In response to this corrosive mentality, Paul's logic is that if we learn to fear God it will drive out lesser fears.

In effect, the apostle poses the question: 'Who do you really work for?' Even if the job is stultifying and soul-destroying, the Christian is free to approach it with vigour. It is not a matter of pleasing some unpredictable line manager, but a question of pleasing the God who loves us and sent his Son to save us. Those further up the chain of command may be inconsiderate, or even vindictive, but if you are a Christian you don't work for them anyway. If we can see our work as a calling from God, something that we do at the express wish of Jesus Christ, it can take the edge off difficult industrial relations. (I once worked for a headmaster who refused me leave of absence to attend my grandfather's funeral.) You may heartily dislike the boss too, and sometimes for good reason, but you are not ultimately answerable to him. It is not only a great challenge to know that 'We must all appear before the judgement seat of Christ, that each one may receive the things done in the body, according to what he has done, whether good or bad' (2 Cor. 5:10); it is also a great comfort. The boss did not give his life for you; Jesus did. Whose disapproval matters most? Whose commitment is the more guaranteed?

The Christian slave is free to work hard (3:23)

Verse 23 follows on naturally from verse 22. If we are answerable **'to the Lord and not to men'**, there is no need to skimp on the job in order to get back at a vindictive boss. The word translated **'heartily'** is a Greek word that means 'from the soul'. The Christian slave then and the believing employee now ought to bring this quality to **'whatever'** they do, including the things that seem trivial, pointless, or just unpleasant. Our head of department may not be worth it, but our heavenly Master is. Many of us have learned from experience that 'A soft answer turns away wrath' (Prov. 15:1). Respond to anger in a calm and gentle way, and you may well defuse it. In the same way, dependability and hard work will often disarm a fault-finding overseer.

In the ancient world, the well-to-do classes were always on their guard against the possibility of a slave revolt. In the two centuries before the birth of Jesus, the Roman Empire expanded rapidly by absorbing neighbouring territories and enslaving vast numbers of foreigners. Not surprisingly, the slaves sometimes snapped, armed themselves and went on the rampage. One such outburst was led by a man named Spartacus. In a similar way, management in Britain became very nervous of organized labour in the late 1970s. The phrase, 'Management must have the right to manage,' became the slogan for a macho, confrontational approach to solving industrial disputes by overwhelming the opposition. It probably arose because of a well-founded suspicion that the trade unions did not play fair.

On a personal level, while there is nothing we can do to prevent a peevish employer being difficult, we are free not to rise to the bait, and sometimes, if not always, a willing attitude, hard work and dependability will remove an employer's suspicion that we are just like the rest, out to achieve maximum gains for a minimum of effort.

The Christian slave is free from exploitation (3:24-25)

A contented workforce needs incentive and recognition. A first-century slave could be tempted to feel something along these lines: 'However much I try, it makes no difference. There's no pleasing him. My contribution is not appreciated.' Before the collieries were nationalized in the United Kingdom in 1947, industrial relationships in most British coalfields came close to being venomous, because the miners were convinced that their skill, courage and commitment counted for nothing. The colliery owners did not want men with aspirations, hopes, dreams and feelings; they simply wanted hands.

And if the boss does have favourites, if you get passed over for promotion and your hard work and loyalty are not valued, then, as a Christian, you can take the long view. Our effort will be rewarded. We may have missed out in the here and now, but **'From the Lord you will receive the reward of the inheritance.'** Even if the movers and shakers ignore your loyal commitment, **'You serve the Lord Christ'** (3:24). How many first-century slaves do you suppose ever heard the words, 'Well done, good and faithful servant' (Matt. 25:21), until they got to glory? Some bosses today will lay on the praise with a trowel, but the attempt at manipulation is easily spotted. Remember then that 'God is not unjust to forget your work and labour of love which you have shown toward his name...' (Heb. 6:10). Whatever others might do, he won't exploit you. There will be recognition, appreciation and greater rewards than these.

It also has to be said that harsh slave-owners and unfair employers will also receive an appropriate reward. They will not get away with it. **'He who does wrong will be repaid for what he has done, and there is no partiality'** with God (3:25). Christian slaves must have drawn much comfort from the stories of Joseph and Daniel. It is possible to serve God when you have no freedom of manoeuvre and you are trapped in uncongenial surroundings. Your circumstances may not have been what you would have chosen, but Jesus knows, and he won't forget.

The Christian master's servitude (4:1)

There was at least one Christian slave-owner in Colosse, a man named Philemon. If you read the short letter that Paul wrote to him, you will discover that a runaway slave of his, named Onesimus, had been converted. Philemon was now going to have to think of his slave in a new way. While the two men were at opposite ends of the social spectrum, the fact that both had put their trust in Christ for salvation meant that they were spiritual equals. Within the church, if not in society or in the home, the old distinctions were now meaningless. (I once heard a testimony from a former soldier who, after his conversion, had become a military chaplain.[2] While in the army he had never risen higher than the modest rank of corporal. He told how he had recently found himself presiding at the Lord's Table and one of the servers had been a general.)

Paul, however, was not merely suggesting that Christian masters should treat Christian slaves decently. There should be fairness and consideration for all. There is a message here for all those who have responsibility for people who are lower in the hierarchy. In modern terms, fair and honest treatment covers a wide range of issues, all the way from fair pay, sensible hours, holiday and pension provision, to union recognition and personal courtesy. Even the chairman of the board is not at the top of the food chain. Paul's words, **'You also have a Master'**, ought to serve as a reminder that no one reaches a point so high up the tree that he ceases to be accountable. 'He who does wrong will be repaid for what he has done' (3:25). Philemon in Colosse needed to grasp that all Christians are servants. However elevated our income or status, we are as much servants of Jesus as the person on the lowest rung of the ladder. Our role model is one who took 'the form of a bondservant' (Phil. 2:7). He himself is a good master and those in authority must strive to be like him.

One excellent example of this principle in action is a middle-ranking Roman officer called a centurion, whom we meet in Luke 7:1-10. He got in touch with Jesus because his servant was 'sick and ready to die' (Luke 7:2). He deserves our attention for two reasons. The first was his attitude to his servant. This is not obvious from most English translations, but he referred to him as 'my boy' (Luke 7:7). The second was that he understood his own place in the pecking order: 'I … am a man placed under authority' (Luke 7:8). This tells us not only that he knew where he stood in the chain of command, but also that he had seen something in Jesus that made him recognize that he was his to command. Who would object to working for a boss like that?

Conclusion

In all human relationships there is a chronic tendency to be self-serving. This often shows itself in the way that we impose conditions. We will fulfil our side of the bargain only when the other party has done the same. Did some slaves in Colosse say, in effect, 'I will work hard when he treats me fairly'? No doubt heads of household were also thinking, 'Is it any wonder that I'm always picking on him when he never does a stroke of work?' In the modern workplace likewise, whether I find myself on the side of labour or of management, while I may not be able to alter the other fellow's attitude and conduct, I can certainly do something about my own. Christians at work need to remember that ultimately we are all accountable. Those at the top of the ladder are not free to do as they please, and those on the bottom rung work for someone far more understanding and appreciative than many a foreman or chief executive officer.

18.
The new nature and our habits of speech

Please read Colossians 4:2-6

As we consider this passage, it is very important that we do not make a common mistake. Some readers, very much aware that the apostle Paul is approaching the end of this letter, suppose that we have reached the stage where all that remained was for Paul to fill in the gaps. According to that view, the main business of the epistle had been safely covered and what follows is a random jumble of bits and pieces, as though Paul used the last few lines to squeeze in those things that he had failed to mention earlier. In point of fact, however, the apostle still had valuable things to say that were very much part of his main argument. In Colossians 4:2-6 a cogent theme is developed with particular care.

The subject that unites these verses is speech. Given that each Christian is to 'put on' deeds that are appropriate to his identity as a 'new man' (3:12-17), what consequences will this have for the way that he talks, whether to God or to other people? It is also noticeable that Paul's words here fit in with what he has said earlier. We have considered the part that the Christian plays in his local church fellowship and his conduct at home and at work; now, towards the end of this section, we can learn from Paul as he outlines the believer's responsibility to those outside the Christian community.

Speaking to God (4:2-4)

Paul wanted to encourage his readers to strive for excellence in prayer (4:2). He did so by making a number of observations about the character of true prayer.

1. Prayer involves hard work

In the first place, true prayer is intense and persistent. The phrase **'continue earnestly'** translates a Greek expression which focuses on the idea that prayer is work, and as such it is both strenuous and dogged. Prayer involves sweat, commitment and unflagging effort. It would be worth asking ourselves how far we see things from Paul's perspective. Has the modern church retained his conviction that prayer must necessarily include an element of hard work? We should not be surprised at this. Jesus' parables of the persistent widow (Luke 18:1-8) and the friend at midnight (Luke 11:5-10) both urge believers to settle in for a campaign of intense, persevering prayer that will not be denied. After all, God is not as flinty and unrelenting as a corrupt judge, or as unresponsive as a sleepy neighbour. He is the loving Father who cares for his children, the tender Shepherd who gave his life for the sheep and who calls them by name.

An earlier generation of Christians used to describe this kind of prayer as 'wrestling with God', thinking no doubt of Jacob's encounter with God at Peniel (Gen. 32:22-32). How often have we approached God with Jacob's relentless determination: 'I will not let you go unless you bless me'? (Gen. 32:26). It has to be said that this kind of praying involves a cost. That meeting with God was not exactly a 'quiet time' and Jacob walked away from it with a limp. People who pray with that kind of focus and that kind of determination will find that strange things can happen. Suppose, for instance, that you become affected by Jesus' words in Luke 10:2: 'The harvest truly is great, but the labourers are few; therefore pray the Lord of the harvest to send out labourers into his harvest.' Steel yourself for the possibility that he might answer your prayer by sending you. People who pray can end up in strange places, their plans disrupted and their lives turned upside down. Think of Mary's touching prayer when the angel announced that she would give birth to the Son of God: 'Behold the maidservant of the Lord! Let it be to me according to your word' (Luke 1:38). What followed? She became the mother whose child was conceived out of wedlock and a target for malicious gossip. The Christian cause needs praying men and women as never before, but before you take up this challenge, brace yourself!

Incidentally, when Paul asked the Christians in Rome to pray for him, he asked them to 'strive together' with him (Rom. 15:30). Wrestling with God does not have to be a solitary activity. Believers can pray together, and even when that opportunity is not available to us, the knowledge that others share our heart concerns, and plead with God about them when they can, is a mighty encouragement.

2. Prayer must be characterized by vigilance

True prayer is also **'vigilant'**. Those who offer it are on the alert, wide awake. This is not simply a challenge to make sure that we pray at a time of day when we are at our best. Paul had in mind the Christian's need to be wary. Just as Jesus warned his disciples, 'Watch and pray, lest you enter into temptation,' telling them, 'The spirit indeed is willing, but the flesh is weak' (Matt. 26:41), so Paul too wanted his readers to be aware of their vulnerability. These words in Colossians were first addressed to the members of a local church who had been gullible and had almost allowed it to be taken over by spiritual impostors. Ravenous predators are on the prowl. On the one hand, 'the devil walks about like a roaring lion' (1 Peter 5:8), while, on the other hand, as Paul warned elsewhere, people can spring up within the churches who, although they may have the appearance of sincere Christians, are actually 'savage wolves' who do not spare the flock (Acts 20:29). It seems that praying with our spiritual eyes wide open, scanning the horizon for any sign of danger, is not as common as it ought to be. Some churches that have gone into a sad decline might still be all that they once were if, in days gone by, prayers for the Lord's protection and for a finely tuned spiritual and theological radar had been more in evidence.

3. Prayer involves thanksgiving

Thirdly, we learn here that true prayer is thankful, as all of our praying should be shot through with a note of **'thanksgiving'**. This theme deserves serious consideration. The scope is vast. If we tried to make an inventory of reasons for thanking God, the list would be almost endless. Many of us are familiar with David's words in Psalm 139:

Where can I go from your Spirit?
Or where can I flee from your presence?
If I ascend into heaven, you are there;
If I make my bed in hell, behold, you are there.
If I take the wings of the morning,
And dwell in the uttermost parts of the sea,
Even there your hand shall lead me,
And your right hand shall hold me.
If I say, 'Surely the darkness shall fall on me,'
Even the night shall be light about me;
Indeed, the darkness shall not hide from you,
But the night shines as the day;
The darkness and the light are both alike to you
(Ps. 139:7-12).

These words were written in a spirit of profound thankfulness. The fact that *God is with us wherever we go* is a cause for rejoicing.

We can also thank God for *providing for our needs in all circumstances*. Paul gave thanks for the food that he ate in a ship that was about to be driven onto a rock-bound shore (Acts 27:35).

Great thanks are due *whenever anyone becomes a follower of Jesus*: 'God be thanked that though you were slaves of sin, yet you obeyed from the heart that form of doctrine to which you were delivered. And having been set free from sin, you became slaves of righteousness' (Rom. 6:17-18).

A certain hope for the future should prompt our gratitude too: 'Thanks be to God, who gives us the victory through our Lord Jesus Christ' (1 Cor. 15:57).

In the same way, *God's covenant faithfulness* deserves a song of thanksgiving. If all things are working together for our good and nothing can separate us from the love of Christ (Rom. 8:28,39), we should be more than grateful, and our praying ought to show it.

4. Prayer should have an evangelistic thrust

Paul was also concerned that the prayers of his friends in Colosse should be mission-minded (4:3-4), that they should have an evangelistic thrust. This is apparent in the way that he requested prayer for himself and his colleagues. (The reference to **'us'** in verse 3 probably includes Timothy, mentioned in 1:1, and also a number of people mentioned from verse 10 onwards — Aristarchus, Mark, Jesus called Justus, and Epaphras.) Neither Paul nor his closest colleagues were beyond the need for prayer. And, in particular, Paul requested prayer that **'God would open a door ... for the word'** (4:3). Paul, writing from prison, did not so much want the Lord to open doors to get him out as to open up a way for the Christian message.

Sometimes the phrase 'open door' suggests a priceless, not-to-be-missed opportunity. Something of this sort prompted Paul to stay in Ephesus longer than he had originally intended: 'For a great and effective door has opened to me, and there are many adversaries' (1 Cor. 16:9).

Another dimension deserves to be considered. This is very graphic language. The apostle is suggesting that, until God changes things, the human personality is bolted and barred against the gospel. John Bunyan was not being fanciful when, in his book *The Holy War*, he portrayed man as a city under siege, with all the senses like massive gates stubbornly holding the truth at bay. But we remember that the Lord opened Lydia's heart (Acts 16:14), and he can open hearts in first-century prisons or anywhere in the cynical postmodern West. Do you feel that, when you try to share the gospel with others, it is as though steel shutters with huge 'no entry' signs bar the minds of your friends? We must pray for one another so that God would clothe our words and witness with the kind of power that will penetrate these barriers of the mind.

Paul certainly wanted prayer so that he might become an increasingly effective communicator. It was his calling to **'speak the mystery of Christ'** (4:3) — that is, to explain a message that is completely beyond human understanding unless God breaks into otherwise closed minds. He needed God's help in two important areas.

The first concerned his longing to make his message **'manifest'** (4:4), or plain and obvious. Communication that is not clear and transparent is bad communication and the message of the gospel is too important to be obscure. A preacher who leaves people confused is a bad preacher.

Secondly, Paul wanted to speak as he **'ought'**, to fulfil his calling. For this he needed the prayers of his friends. This admission is very winning. Far from presenting himself as a man of steel, impervious to the difficulties experienced by ordinary mortals, Paul needed help. Every preacher and evangelist does. Mr Spurgeon once said that the reason why his ministry was one long, sustained harvest of souls was that 'My people pray for me'. The pastor who can say what Spurgeon said is a happy man. But then, all believers are involved in telling others the good news. Not one of us is so competent and effective that we can do without the prayers of our brothers and sisters.

Speaking to others (4:5-6)

Paul's logic in these verses cannot be faulted. If we want to speak to others about God and his message of reconciling love, our efforts will carry little weight unless we first speak to God about them.

1. The plight of those to whom we are speaking

The apostle's description of those who are not yet Christians is heartbreaking. They are **'those who are outside'** (4:5). This is both poignant and desperately sad. Most of us have at least some experience of what it feels like to be an outsider, to be left out of the charmed circle of those who matter. It is grievous indeed when it is made clear that you are not welcome and that you don't belong. I remember some wistful words: 'That church is full of cliques and I'm not in any of them.' But what could be worse than being outside the Christian community?

There is a terrible irony at work here. In this life, many people find Christians embarrassing and exclude them from their friendships, yet they themselves are on the outside of the only society that truly matters. And they exclude themselves.

They have repeatedly spurned the invitation that Christ extends to attend his great banquet: 'Come, for all things are now ready' (Luke 14:17). There was a welcome for them, but they wanted none of it and dressed their refusal up in flimsy excuses. And many of those who are on the outside now will be on the outside for ever, consigned to the darkness outside (Matt. 25:30). The phrase 'outer darkness' is enough to make anyone tremble. What a picture of eternity! On the inside, there is light and warmth, joy and acceptance; there is Jesus and his love; while outside there is misery that cannot be mended and loss that cannot be retrieved. Surely, then, if we know anything of Paul's outlook, we want outsiders to become insiders.

Indeed, I have something to say to everyone reading this book who is not yet a decided follower of Jesus. Sooner than let your alienation from God become permanent, I plead with you, come inside, where there is acceptance with God and the forgiveness of Jesus. Why stay on the outside a moment longer?

2. The kind of life that gives credibility to our words

And surely those of us who are Christians want to share the gospel effectively? In that case, our first great need is personal credibility. This is what Paul had in mind when he urged his readers to **'walk in wisdom'** (4:5). This is a plea for believers to live integrated, wholesome Christian lives that do not detract from our message. Sadly, it is possible to do the very opposite and undermine our witness. There are a variety of ways in which believers can be foolish.

One of these is *materialism.* 'Having food and clothing, with these we shall be content. But those who desire to be rich fall into temptation and a snare, and into many foolish and harmful lusts which drown men in destruction and perdition' (1 Tim. 6:8-9). An outsider will not be impressed by a materialistic Christian. Where is the difference?

Another barrier to effective evangelism is *legalism*. A religion which appears to be little more than a hidebound obsession with pernickety minutiae does not attract those who are desperate for an experience of the love of God. Paul chided the 'foolish Galatians' (Gal. 3:1) for adding unnecessary rules to the simplicity of the gospel! Think long and hard about how you carry off those self-imposed rules. Had you considered that the outsider might not so much stand in awe of a man of principle as feel unnerved by the obsessions of a crank?

The antidote to folly is to seek wisdom: 'The fear of the LORD is the beginning of wisdom, and the knowledge of the Holy One is understanding' (Prov. 9:10). But how are we to acquire such wisdom? Be frank with God about your need of it! 'If any of you lacks wisdom, let him ask of God, who gives to all liberally and without reproach, and it will be given to him' (James 1:5). 'Let the word of Christ dwell in you richly in all wisdom, teaching and admonishing one another in psalms and hymns and spiritual songs, singing with grace in your hearts to the Lord' (3:16).

To sum up so far, the key to effective evangelism is not so much to learn certain techniques of communication, but to work at being a godly person whose character will add credibility to his message.

3. A sense of urgency

If we are to be like Paul, we will also have a sense of urgency. **'Redeeming the time'** (4:5) means that we become aware that time is in short supply. Moments fly; windows of opportunity close, and unless we seize the day, the possibility of saying something that will count for eternity will soon have passed us by.

4. The way in which we speak to others

When we do speak to others, our conversation is to be both gracious and salty (4:6). Consider for a moment what would happen if our language was the opposite, if it was ungracious and insipid. Communicate a message of love in scolding or superior tones, and people will feel resentful on the one hand and patronized on the other. A kindly, tender and loving message deserves to be conveyed with warmth and gentleness. No one was ever nagged into the kingdom. **'Salt'**, of course, can sting when applied to an open wound. The idea here is that there is a place for confrontation and challenge in our communication of the gospel provided that the element of grace is kept in view. Grace will prevent direct and challenging words from becoming too abrasive. Salt will prevent kind and tender words from becoming limp and sentimental.

Paul ends this section with a note of encouragement for timid souls. We are not all equally good at initiating conversations about spiritual things. Some of us end up feeling guilty and inadequate. We should remind ourselves that not every first-century Christian was a Paul or an Epaphras, a public herald of the gospel. Furthermore, in a world where people are desperate for significance and have been sold short by the false gods of materialism and pleasure-seeking, they will not be able to help asking questions. Let us pray for one another so that when the questions come, we will have the grace and saltiness to **'answer each one'** (4:6). 'But sanctify the Lord God in your hearts, and always be ready to give a defence to everyone who asks you a reason for the hope that is in you, with meekness and fear' (1 Peter 3:15).

Conclusion

In ordinary human relationships, few things are more de-
structive than thoughtless or malicious words. The apostle
James reminds us that the influence of the tongue is out of all
proportion to its size, like the bit in a horse's mouth, or the
rudder that steers a huge vessel (James 3:3,4). In Proverbs
18:21 we are told that 'Death and life are in the power of the
tongue.' The same tongue that preaches the gospel to good
effect may, on occasion, belittle someone and leave him with
a crushed spirit. The same tongue may offer praise to God
and hurtful sarcasm to loved ones, friends and colleagues
who are made in his image (James 3:9). It is therefore of the
utmost importance that those who have 'put on the new man'
(3:10), and now mean to put on the kind of behaviour that
goes with their new identity, should seek to bring their
tongues under control, or, as James puts it, to 'tame' their
tongues (James 3:7-8), so that there is a harmony between
the way that we speak to God and the way that we speak to
others.

19.
A capacity for friendship

Please read Colossians 4:7-18

We come now to the final section of this epistle. One thing stands out from these verses: the number of people who are mentioned. Only in Romans 16 do we find a longer list than this one. This in itself makes a telling point that we should not miss. Although Paul was under arrest pending trial in Rome when he wrote these words, he was not alone. He was at the centre of an extensive network of friends and helpers. Paul was a man with a capacity for friendship. He had a warm heart and a big heart.

This point needs to be made because the idea has gained ground in recent years that the apostle was a severe and unattractive man who inspired respect rather than affection. It is even suggested that the Christian movement took a wrong turning once Paul the Pharisee got hold of it because, unlike Jesus, whose dominant characteristic was love, Paul was a man who overawed and drove people, whereas Jesus won their hearts. It is surprising how persistent this idea is when all the evidence is against it. When, for example, after two years in Ephesus, Paul departed for Jerusalem, the believers all gathered for what became a tearful farewell: 'Then they all wept freely, and fell on Paul's neck and kissed him, sorrowing most of all for the words which he spoke, that they would see his face no more. And they accompanied him to the ship' (Acts 20:37-38). If Paul had really been an austere and demanding character, surely they would have been quietly relieved that he was going?

Also, by emphasizing the bonds that linked him to the church in Colosse, Paul could prove beyond doubt that he had an accurate picture of their situation and that he had a right to express his concerns about the predatory newcomers who had almost seized control there. The modern reader will also note that we are given a number of snapshots of fine first-century Christians. We can seek God's grace to emulate Paul; we can also try to copy his friends.

Two messengers (4:7-9)

First we meet two men who would soon be travelling together from Rome to Colosse on Paul's behalf.

1. Tychicus

The first, Tychicus, whose name means 'fortunate' or 'lucky', was to be the bearer of this very letter. He was probably a native of Ephesus and is mentioned five times in the New Testament. We first meet him in Acts 20:4, when Paul, on his third missionary journey, was on his way to Jerusalem, taking gifts from the churches in Europe to help Jewish believers caught up in a terrible famine. Paul called at Ephesus en route and Tychicus went with him, staying with Paul during all his travels up to the time of writing, when he was in Rome during his first imprisonment there. Tychicus had gone back and forth across the eastern Mediterranean in the apostle's company. He was clearly a man of outstanding spiritual calibre. At one point, Paul had considered using him as a stand-in for Titus, the leader of the churches in Crete (Titus 3:12).

By now the two men had been together for four years and Tychicus was entrusted with a perilous mission. To get from Rome to Colosse he would first have to cross the Italian peninsula on foot, then make the first of two sea-crossings over the Adriatic to Illyricum, modern Albania. This would be followed by another long slog on foot along the Egnatian Way through Macedonia until he reached the port of Thessalonica on the Aegean Sea. A second sea crossing would take him to Ephesus on the coast of Asia Minor. Colosse lay a hundred miles inland from Ephesus in the Lycus Valley. It would be long, time-consuming, potentially hazardous and exhausting, and Tychicus had a precious burden to carry. He had to get the letters we know as Colossians and Philemon to their destinations and, since he went by way of Ephesus, it is highly likely that he delivered that epistle as well (Eph. 6:21). There was also a letter from Paul to the believers in nearby Laodicea that has not survived.

Modern Christians owe a great deal to the fact that Tychicus carried out his mission successfully. Countless believers over twenty centuries of the Christian era have been stirred by the picture of the Christian soldier in Ephesians 6:10-20, taken to heights of worship by the exalted description of Christ in Colossians 1:15-20 and moved by the touching appeal to Christian forgiveness in the tender letter to Philemon. We owe all of that, in the providence of God, to the fact that a first-century Christian was faithful to his charge and resolutely travelled hundreds of miles in conditions that would leave an experienced modern traveller balking at the hardship and danger of it all.

We know something of his quality from a number of phrases that Paul used of him. He was a **'beloved brother'** (4:7). I suspect that Paul wanted his readers to understand that this was not merely his own estimate of Tychicus, but a conclusion that was widely shared among those who knew him. He was also a **'faithful minister'**. This does not mean a 'minister' in the restricted modern sense of the word, a church elder set aside for the ministry of the Word and prayer and freed from the need to earn his living in some other way. Here **'minister'** translates a Greek word, which means 'servant' in a general sense.[1] At the same time we should note that Paul used exactly the same word to describe his own ministry (see 1:23,25). Paul thought of Tychicus as being as much a 'minister' as he was. It is clear that Tychicus was no untried novice, but a man who had already proved that he could be entrusted with a great task. The third phrase used to describe him, **'fellow servant in the Lord'**, means that Paul saw Tychicus as a man like himself, a bond-slave of Jesus Christ. Their gifts may have differed, but at the level of commitment their two hearts beat as one.

2. Onesimus

Tychicus would not be travelling alone. His companion was Onesimus, a runaway slave who had been converted in Rome. He was going home. Paul's phrase, **'who is one of you'** (4:9), tells us that Onesimus was from Colosse himself. (It was also a gentle hint to his Colossian readers that Paul had inside information about the situation there.) In one sense, Onesimus was going back to face the music, but Paul's short letter to his master, Philemon, himself a Christian, was intended to smooth the path with a tender appeal for forgiveness, given that Onesimus was now a changed man, a wonderful example of the power of God. He had once been feckless and irresponsible, dealing with problems by running away from them, but now he was **'a faithful and beloved brother'** (4:9). Has your life been a waste up till now? Once God goes to work that need never be the end of the story.

Three Jewish Christians (4:10-11)

At this point Paul included greetings from a number of Christians who were closely involved with him but who would not be making the journey to Colosse. The first three were **'of the circumcision'** (4:11), Christians of Jewish extraction. Note Paul's wistful observation that these were his **'only fellow workers for the kingdom'** from that background. The fact that the bulk of the Jewish people at that time had not responded in faith to Israel's Messiah was something that Paul felt very keenly (see Rom. 9:1-5).

1. Aristarchus

First we meet Aristarchus, a Jew of the Diaspora born in Thessalonica. He had already learned that following Jesus was no easy option, having been seized by the rioting mob in Ephesus that resented the way that Paul's preaching had undermined the flourishing trade in silver trinkets of the goddess Diana (Acts 19:29). There is a strong likelihood that he had accompanied Paul on his journey to Jerusalem and then on to Rome. Paul's description of him as his **'fellow prisoner'** (4:10) says a great deal about this man. It was not that he had been arrested along with Paul and held pending trial as he was. It was rather than he had taken up residence in the prison voluntarily in order to be a helper and companion to Paul. He was in prison because he chose to be, like the Moravian missionaries in the eighteenth century who deliberately sold themselves into slavery in the West Indies so that they could share the gospel with the black slaves. Aristarchus understood the force of Jesus' words: 'I was naked and you clothed me; I was sick and you visited me; I was in prison and you came to me' (Matt. 25:36). He was an outstanding example of practical compassion at work.

2. Mark

The Mark mentioned in verse 10 is no less than John Mark, the author of Mark's Gospel. His inclusion here is both fascinating and thrilling. At one time he had proved a great disappointment to Paul. On the apostle's first missionary journey, at Perga in Pamphylia, a much younger Mark had deserted Paul and Barnabas (Acts 13:13). This in turn had led to a parting of the ways between Paul and Barnabas (Acts 15:37-39). Barnabas wanted to give Mark a second chance, whereas Paul feared that he would prove a liability. Was there any reason to suppose that there would not be a second failure of nerve? The note here that Mark was **'the cousin of Barnabas'** may help to explain the patience of that good man. When the grace of God is at work, there is hope for cowards. Mark had close links with the apostle Peter, a man who had himself been restored to spiritual usefulness after a shameful display of cowardice (1 Peter 5:13). At any rate, time had passed and Mark had built himself a reputation as a steady and useful Christian. Paul had no lingering suspicions of him and clearly thought that he deserved a welcome in Colosse as a believer in good standing. By the time of Paul's final imprisonment, when 2 Timothy was written, Mark had become one of his most stalwart and valuable companions: 'He is useful to me for ministry' (2 Tim. 4:11).

3. Jesus called Justus

We know little about the third character. Jesus is the Greek form of the Hebrew Yehoshua (Yahweh saves) and Justus is a Latin surname, meaning 'righteous'. We have no way of knowing whether this name was an expression of pious aspiration, or whether it was given to him because his character deserved it. At any rate, we know that, like John

Mark, he had **'proved to be a comfort'** to Paul (4:11) and had helped to put new heart into him.

Three Gentile Christians (4:12-14)

1. Epaphras

The next of Paul's associates to be mentioned was Epaphras. Again, the phrase, **'one of you'** (4:12) tells us not only that Epaphras was a citizen of Colosse himself, but also that Paul wanted the believers there to know that he had reached his conclusions about the state of the church on the basis of sound information. As we have seen, Epaphras was in fact the founder of the churches in the Lycus Valley. He was probably the current pastor of the church in Colosse and had made the long journey to Rome to seek help and guidance once he had realized the extent of the threat posed by the newcomers.

Paul's generous tribute to this good man was partly intended to bolster his standing within the church. The new teachers had probably damned his teaching with faint praise, and him along with it, arguing that those who longed for real depth and maturity in their Christian experience would not be content to remain with the frankly minimal gospel that Epaphras had brought to the Lycus Valley. It is ironic, therefore, that Paul mentioned his **'great zeal'** for the three churches (4:13). This showed itself in fervent prayer (4:12). The phrase **'labouring fervently'** translates a Greek word that is also the root of our word 'agony'. Epaphras' prayer life cost him sweat, toil and pain. But it is the content of his prayer for the Christians in Colosse that makes the accusations of the new teachers so unjust. He prayed that the believers in his home town might **'stand perfect and complete in all the will of God'**. To argue that this man knew nothing of Christian fulness and spiritual maturity was a travesty.

2. Luke

Luke (4:14), the author of the Gospel that bears his name and also of the book of Acts, is mentioned by name only three times in the New Testament but was often involved in the action. The passages in the book of Acts where he employs the word 'we' tell us that he was a frequent companion of Paul, and the affectionate description of him as **'the beloved physician'** tells us that he was greatly valued by the apostle.

3. Demas

Reference is also made in passing to a man named Demas (4:14). This is very poignant. The next time we hear of this man, he had defected: 'Demas has forsaken me, having loved this present world, and has departed for Thessalonica…' (2 Tim. 4:10). It was no small privilege to have been a trusted associate of the apostle Paul, yet the time came when a man who had once walked alongside a spiritual giant lost the inward battle for possession of his heart. The daily call to deny oneself and follow Christ demands reserves of toughness and consistency that only God can give, and Demas gave way to the pull of the world.

When Paul wrote to the believers in Colosse the sense of betrayal and disappointed hopes still lay in the future, but there is a solemn reminder here that the real test of a Christian is staying power. Does he or she last the course? This would be an appropriate point to reflect carefully on our own spiritual weakness. It is disturbing to consider the possibility that someone who thanks God for us now may one day be sorrowing over what we have become.

Conclusion

Mercifully, there was only one Demas. On the whole Paul's friends were an impressive group. It says a great deal for the apostle himself that he attracted people of such sterling quality.

Some of the other references in this passage are so brief that they leave us with tantalizing questions. Who was Archippus? What was the ministry that he needed encouragement to fulfil? (4:17). Who was Nymphas, who hosted a church in his home? (4:15). There is some uncertainty as to whether this generous Christian was a man at all. The manuscripts are divided between Nymphas, a man's name, and Nympha, the feminine version. On balance it seems most likely that the ESV, NASB and the NKJV footnote are correct and that Paul wanted to thank God for the hospitality of a believing lady called Nympha. We ought to note in passing that the overwhelming bulk of first-century churches met in homes. Purpose-built church buildings were as yet unknown and would have been impractical when we consider the poverty of many early Christians and the ever-present threat of persecution. A Christian with a spacious home who was willing to let the church meet there could be a real encouragement and blessing.[2]

Amid all the detail, the one thing that we must not miss is that, as well as telling us something about Paul's associates, these verses say a great deal about Paul himself. We not only see his evident enjoyment of people and his care for them, but it is also clear that he shared his ministry. There was nothing of the control freak about him. His use of the word **'fellow'** is very telling. Tychicus was his 'fellow servant' (4:7), Aristarchus his 'fellow prisoner' (4:10) and John Mark and Jesus Justus were his 'fellow workers' (4:10-11). Paul did not want people to work *for* him but *with* him. Some prominent Christian workers have been quite the opposite.

His loyalty to Epaphras also stands out. It pained him that this true-hearted servant of Christ had not received his due among the people who had benefited from his ministry. It is also worth noting what impressed him in other people and asking ourselves what Paul would have thought of us.

We can see from verse 18 that, as he brought this letter to a close, Paul stopped dictating and wrote the final greeting, or **'salutation'**, with his **'own hand'** (4:18). This was his usual practice (2 Thess. 3:17). It seems that he needed to guard against forged letters circulating around the churches that falsely claimed his authority.

The touching request, **'Remember my chains'**, is a plea for the sympathy, emotional support and, by implication, the prayers of the believers in Colosse. Paul asks them to recognize that the man whose greatest longing was to carry the gospel to parts of the world where it was quite unknown was confined like a caged bird.

Finally, the letter ends, as it began, by commending Paul's readers to the grace of God. Those who cherish this letter today will never get beyond the need for the grace that saves us, keeps us and will one day lead us to our eternal home.

Part 2:
Philemon

Introduction to Philemon

In the first part of this book we have been looking together at the letter that the apostle Paul wrote to the church in Colosse. Now we turn to a short letter that was sent at the same time and by the same messenger. As we saw in chapter 19, Paul, under house arrest in Rome, had entrusted the delivery of the letter that we know as Colossians to a man named Tychicus. He was also given the responsibility of delivering this letter. It concerns two first-century believers. It was intended for one member of the church in Colosse and related to another person from the same town. It is a highly personal letter written from one Christian to another, from the apostle Paul to a man named Philemon. The two main characters were Philemon himself and his runaway but now returning slave, Onesimus. To understand the epistle it is worth looking at each of these characters in turn.

The two principal characters

1. Philemon

Philemon probably became a Christian through contact with Paul. This would explain Paul's aside in verse 19: 'You owe me even your own self.' We cannot be certain how this came about. At the time of writing, Paul had never been to Colosse, so the two men must have met somewhere else. Most commentators opt for Ephesus as the likeliest place for a meeting. Ephesus was the nearest port to Colosse. Given that Paul was active there for three years and that Philemon may have been a businessman, perhaps the Colossian trader did learn about the gospel from the apostle in that bustling commercial centre.

We shall examine the character of Philemon in the following chapter, but it is clear from the letter that he was a man of means, and that he was a family man whose home was a place where the people of God gathered for worship.

2. Onesimus

This brings us to the person who is the subject of this letter, a man named Onesimus, a native of Colosse and a runaway slave. We don't know why he absconded. Perhaps he simply longed for freedom and saw an opportunity to make his escape. There is a hint in verse 18 that he might have financed his new life by stealing from his master, Philemon.

Rome is a long way from Colosse, but the runaway had found his way there, no doubt hoping to merge with the crowds in the capital. It was probably a wretched existence. A third of the population of the empire was made up of slaves. Enough of them decamped for bounty hunters to make a good living tracking down the runaways and bringing them back to face the music. Punishments were harsh. A slave-owner could do as he liked with a recalcitrant slave. Some runaways were crucified; others were branded on the forehead with the letter 'F' for *'fugitivus'*. It must have been a nerve-wracking affair, always looking over his shoulder, knowing that he could betray his origins with a slip of the tongue. (In the same way, modern young people who run away to the big city can find their dreams evaporate as they live in squalor on the fringes of the underworld.)

Onesimus also found, like the prodigal son in Jesus' parable, that you can't run away from God. Try as you might, you only succeed in running into him. Once the grace of God has you in its sights, there is ultimately no escape. At some point during his stay in Rome, Onesimus met Paul and was converted. Was this, from the human point of view, pure coincidence? Or did this young fugitive, in deep spiritual turmoil, come to himself and seek Paul out, having heard of him from Philemon? We cannot know for sure, but it is clear that he became a changed man. Paul now wrote of him in glowing terms. He had become like a 'son' to the apostle (10). Losing him would be like losing his 'own heart' (12). He was now a 'beloved brother' (16). (The same phrase is used of him in Colossians 4:9.) A similar idea is conveyed by way of a pun on his name (11). Onesimus means 'useful' or 'profitable'. It is the kind of patronizing name that people in the ancient world would give to a slave. He had not been useful at all as far as Philemon was concerned but, since his conversion, he had now become very useful to Paul.

It is a delightful story, one more example of the way that the gospel changes lives and that unpromising human material is transformed into something beautiful for Jesus. The story of Onesimus is repeated every day of the week. You might well know more than one Onesimus. You might even be one.

Why read the epistle to Philemon?

This epistle has a fascination all its own. At its heart there is a theme that is vital for all Christians — that of forgiveness. Paul wanted his friend Philemon to act as a model of this Christian grace.

We discover, as the letter unfolds, that Paul intended to send Onesimus back to Philemon. He would be safe with Tychicus as his escort. (A runaway slave on his own would have been enormously vulnerable.) Paul wanted Philemon to take him back, not grudgingly, or on probation, but with open arms. The key phrase is: 'Receive him as you would me' (17). We can well imagine the kind of welcome that Paul would have been given in Philemon's home!

1. Christians are forgiven people

The subject of forgiveness is of compelling interest to all Christians because we ourselves are a forgiven people. None of us gained a stake in the love of God on merit. What defines our identity is the fact that we all have a moment in our past where we came before God with nothing to offer him but guilt and shame. In effect, we said, 'I will arise and go to my father, and will say to him, "Father, I have sinned against heaven and before you…"' (Luke 15:18). Indeed, our need for pardon is constant. Just as we must ask God for our daily bread, so we must also ask for daily forgiveness.

2. Christians are required to be forgiving people

We are not in heaven yet and we all offend in many things. Forgiveness is an ongoing necessity in all our relationships. Every Christian marriage, family and local church is a community where no one can escape the need to ask for pardon and no one escapes the need to give it. Paul had already impressed this on the believers in Colosse: 'Therefore, as the elect of God, holy and beloved, put on tender mercies, kindness, humility, meekness, long-suffering; bearing with one another, and forgiving one another, if anyone has a complaint against another; even as Christ forgave you, so you also must do' (Col. 3:12-13).

Indeed, when Christians are slow to forgive it calls into question their own experience of God's pardoning love. Jesus' parable of the unforgiving servant (Matt. 18:21-35) shows how monstrous it is for people who have been released from an enormous load of guilt to be reluctant to pardon much more trifling offences from their fellow human beings. Few things bring the cause of God into more disrepute than Christians who begrudge reconciliation. A refusal to forgive causes damage in a number of areas.

First of all, the person who will not forgive puts the person who wronged him in prison and throws away the key. There is to be no light at the end of the tunnel, nothing but ongoing recrimination. But it is not just the effect on the other person that is tragic. The one who refuses marcy puts himself in prison. He is locked up in a past where he cannot leave his hurt behind. His grievance is like a ball and chain round his ankle. Pardon withheld keeps the pain alive.

Secondly, unwillingness to forgive helps encourage the growth of what Hebrews 12:15 calls a 'root of bitterness'. The growth of affection and mutual regard is stifled. Relationships wither because barriers of mutual suspicion grow up, built on carefully nursed grievances.

Thirdly, a reluctance to be reconciled gives the enemy an opportunity to exploit: '"Be angry, and do not sin": do not let the sun go down on your wrath, nor give place to the devil' (Eph. 4:26-27). Satan is always on the prowl as it is. Refusing to forgive opens the door to him and bids him walk through it.

Fourthly, an unrelenting attitude will mar our relationship with God: 'If you forgive men their trespasses, your heavenly Father will also forgive you. But if you do not forgive men their trespasses, neither will your Father forgive your trespasses' (Matt. 6:14-15). God is very merciful. He delights in it. Small wonder, then, that estrangement grows between a pardoning God and professing believers who are hard and unyielding.

3. The world at large is crying out for forgiveness

In popular culture the hero is the person who refuses to be pushed around and who gives as good as he gets. We are surrounded by people who are deeply unhappy because they cannot let go of old quarrels, or who long to be back on the old footing with a friend who loves a nursed grievance more than the memory of happier days. In England in 2004, a man was murdered in what was once a coal-mining district in Nottinghamshire partly because neither he nor his murderer could put behind them the bitterness that occurred when they were on opposite sides twenty years earlier, during the coal strike in 1984. In several parts of the world there is stalemate because the participants in an ancient quarrel cannot forget it and the search for revenge is pursued with ferocious intensity. Take the policy of 'an eye for an eye' to its limits, and we all end up blind. Perhaps as never before, the world is aching for a demonstration of the power of forgiveness.

20.
The kind of man who can forgive

Please read Philemon 1-7

Greetings (1-3)

Paul began his letter to Philemon in his customary manner, with the formula, 'The writer to the reader, greetings.' (For an explanation of this practice, which was the norm in the ancient world, see the comments on Colossians 1:1 on page 19.)

On this occasion he made no reference to being an apostle, but referred to himself in a very affecting manner as **'a prisoner of Christ Jesus'** (1). Whenever Paul described himself as a prisoner, he used an expression like this in order to make the point that, while at one level he had been deprived of his liberty by the Roman authorities, he did not really see himself as Caesar's prisoner at all. It had all come about because he belonged to Jesus Christ. Had Christ not taken him captive, there is no reason to suppose that Paul would ever have ended up in a Roman gaol. His incarceration had taken place because he was on active service for a greater monarch than the emperor who sat enthroned in Rome.

Paul may have had another reason for mentioning his imprisonment. His purpose in writing the letter was to request a favour from Philemon, the recipient of the letter. (For more comments on Philemon and the other people mentioned in verse 2, Apphia and Archippus, see below.) It would be all the more difficult for Philemon to refuse this request knowing the apostle's situation. Timothy was with Paul at the time of writing and was therefore included in the greeting.

The actual greeting that Paul used to conclude this opening section, **'Grace to you and peace from God our Father and the Lord Jesus Christ'** (3), is identical to the one that we find in Colossians 1:2 (see comments on that verse on pages 20-22).

A pen portrait of Philemon

Philemon was a man whom Paul valued and appreciated. Phrases such as 'beloved friend' and 'fellow labourer' (1) give us an idea of his measure. Paul valued him as a person and also appreciated his contribution to the spread of the gospel. No doubt Philemon himself was mightily encouraged to receive such a generous tribute from a man like Paul.

1. His home and family

Philemon was *a man of means*. We are told that he owned a house large enough to host gatherings of the church (2). Whether all the believers in Colosse met in his home, or whether other 'house churches' existed in the city, we cannot know for sure.

Philemon was also *a family man*. 'The beloved Apphia' mentioned in verse 2 was probably his wife and Archippus his son. If so, Philemon had a son old enough to have a ministry of his own. We don't know what that ministry was, but in Colossians 4:17 there is a challenge that Archippus should take heed to it and fulfil it. Here, in this epistle, Paul spoke in more encouraging terms, describing the young man as a 'fellow soldier', a comrade in arms for the sake of the gospel. Language of this kind would have made Archippus' pulse quicken. Towards the end of the first of C. S. Lewis' Narnia Chronicles, *The Lion the Witch and the Wardrobe*, a fierce battle was about to take place between the forces of the White Witch and the true Narnians, loyal servants of Aslan, the great golden lion who was the lord and saviour of Narnia and the son of the emperor over the sea. As Aslan deployed his troops, he approached a Narnian lion and said, 'Us lions will fight over here.' Straight away, the other lion felt invincible. He couldn't get over the way that Aslan had spoken of both of them fighting together and kept saying, 'He said, "us lions"!' What would it do for a young Christian worker to be told by no less than the apostle that the two of them were fellow soldiers?

Philemon's home was clearly an attractive place, where the people of God were welcome and both generations were keen to do what they could for Jesus. Christian couples would do well to build homes like that.

2. A man of spiritual calibre

God delights in forgiveness and bestows it freely on those who seek it. And, far from being a weakling who lets himself be pushed around, the person who is most able to forgive is the one who most resembles God. Paul was confident that he could appeal to Philemon to forgive Onesimus because he knew that he was a man of real spiritual calibre. We learn in verses 4-7 that Paul prayed for Philemon and that when he did so, he thanked God for the man that grace had made him.

It is noticeable that Philemon had a heart for Christ and a heart for his people (5). Paul writes of the **'love and faith'** which he had **'toward the Lord Jesus and toward all the**

saints'. We should note in passing that in this context 'faith' does not mean the faith that saves so much as loyal and steadfast commitment. Paul meant that Philemon's love, both for Jesus and his people, was loyal and dependable. These qualities clearly stood out in Philemon's life. Paul heard about these things because others talked about them. No doubt these encouraging reports came from Epaphras, the founder of the church in Colosse, who was in Rome at the time, and perhaps from Onesimus. It must have been wonderfully encouraging for Paul to reflect on the way that a man who had come to faith through his own ministry had become such an impressive Christian. Paul was quite convinced that a man with such an evident love for the Lord and for his fellow believers would not be the type to harbour grudges.

In the same way, we read that Philemon had refreshed **'the hearts of the saints'** (7). We cannot tell exactly how he did this, but it seems likely that he held office in the church. As a well-to-do man he was generous and big-hearted. Surely, Paul reasoned, a person who did not stint on kindness would not withhold reconciliation and stubbornly keep an offender at arm's length?

What Paul desired for Philemon (6)

Paul's prayer for Philemon in verse 6 is difficult to translate. English versions of the Bible render it in a variety of ways. The main idea seems to be that Paul prayed that Philemon would benefit more and more as the quality of his discipleship intensified. The **'sharing'** of his faith mentioned here is not to do with evangelism — sharing the Christian faith with outsiders — but sharing himself with his fellow believers, a sharing in faith and in Christ. Paul prayed, in effect, for a blessed upward spiral, that devotion and Christian character would work to produce more of the same.

The challenge facing Philemon

What does all this have to do with the main thrust of the letter? Paul understood that he was asking a great deal of Philemon. Forgiveness is demanding precisely because it does not come naturally. Our normal response to a slight is to respond in kind. Of course no Christian grace comes naturally. All the fruit of the Spirit is supernatural in origin. There is a sense in which Christian character is all of a piece. In the world of professional football[1] one sometimes encounters players whose skills are unbalanced. I have seen centre forwards who could leap like a salmon and head a ball sweetly, yet on the ground they had two left feet. But the ability to forgive is not something that can be acquired in isolation, as a skill all on its own. Paul could appeal to Philemon because he was a man who strove for excellence in every area of spiritual life. He was a man of well-rounded godliness. His example is a spur to modern Christians not only to learn how to be gentle, long-suffering, tender-hearted and forgiving, but to be outstanding in every area of our walk with God.

Incidentally, we ought to note that the return of Onesimus would present Philemon with another challenge. There was potentially more at stake than the healing of a relationship between two men, one a Christian slave-owner and the other a believing slave. His reaction to one converted slave in particular would give Philemon the opportunity to reflect on his treatment of slaves in general. Would he be able to see that the claims of Christian brotherhood could somehow leap across the enormous social chasm that separated him from his workforce? It is highly likely that a sizeable proportion of believers in the first centuries of the Christian era were slaves. The institution of slavery itself is plainly wrong, but in an age when there was no realistic possibility of overturning it, if men like Philemon who held power could appreciate that in Christ 'There is neither slave nor free' (Gal. 3:28), some of its worst features would have been considerably lessened.

Conclusion

These verses remind us of a sobering fact. We all want forgiveness when we are in the wrong, but it takes a person of rare calibre to be forgiving, and there is more at stake than the act of pardon itself. Philemon was a man of well-rounded godliness. That is precisely why Paul anticipated a favourable outcome for his appeal that his friend should forgive Onesimus. We too shall meet an Onesimus from time to time and be reminded of just how truculent we can be at such times. If we can develop the habit of cultivating all-round Christian maturity in the meantime, forgiveness may not prove quite so hard as it sometimes can.

21.
Why should Christians forgive?

Please read Philemon 8-25

Reasons why Christians must be forgiving people

1. Failure to forgive is a breach of God's law

First of all, Christians who refuse to forgive break the Sixth Commandment. In the Sermon on the Mount, Jesus explained that the commandment not to commit murder goes well beyond the actual act of homicide and concerns the way that we think about other people: 'You have heard that it was said to those of old, "You shall not murder, and whoever murders will be in danger of the judgement." But I say to you that whoever is angry with his brother without a cause shall be in danger of the judgement. And whoever says to his brother, "Raca!" shall be in danger of the council. But whoever says, "You fool!" shall be in danger of hell fire' (Matt. 5:21-22). An unforgiving spirit allows malice to simmer and keeps anger warm. It reviews old grievances and brings them back to boiling point. This mindset often betrays a lack of a sense of proportion. While we are convinced that others should forgive us without delay, on the assumption that our offences against them were trivial, we feel justified in withholding forgiveness from them, on the grounds that their offences against us were monstrous.

2. God has forgiven us

Secondly, forgiveness is imperative among Christians because of the way that God has treated us. If we sin against a fellow believer, that sin is an offence on two levels. We sin against the brother himself and also against the Lord. This latter offence is by far the more serious of the two. When King David sinned against both Bathsheba and her husband, he said to God, 'Against you, you only, have I sinned, and done this evil in your sight...' (Ps. 51:4). Yet if, in the case of a fellow Christian, God has forgiven the greater sin, can we not forgive the lesser?

3. Failure to forgive leads to a breach of fellowship

A failure to forgive others will also mar our fellowship with God: 'For if you forgive men their trespasses, your heavenly Father will also forgive you. But if you do not forgive men their trespasses, neither will your Father forgive your trespasses' (Matt. 6:14-15). When there is a breach between two Christians because one has offended the other, a failure to resolve the matter also creates a breach between the unrelenting party and God. A merciful God is angered by a merciless streak in his servants.

In the same way, a refusal to forgive will also mar our fellowship with other believers. In Jesus' parable of the unforgiving servant a man who had a colossal debt written off treated someone who owed him a trifling sum with overbearing rage. The other servants, who were rightly outraged at his behaviour (Matt. 18:31), reported him to their master. Deny a broken and repentant brother the forgiveness he seeks, and you will disappoint and exasperate other Christians who learn of your refusal to relent.

4. Failure to forgive is a slight on the authority of God

Furthermore, the Christian who will not forgive usurps the authority of God: 'Bless those who persecute you; bless and do not curse. Beloved, do not avenge yourselves, but rather give place to wrath; for it is written, "Vengeance is Mine, I will repay," says the Lord' (Rom. 12:14,19). Withhold forgiveness and, in effect, we accuse God of having lower standards than we do. We are implying that we would have ensured that justice was done!

5. Failure to forgive hinders worship

In addition, bearing grudges renders believers unfit for worship: 'If you bring your gift to the altar, and there remember that your brother has something against you, leave your gift there before the altar, and go your way. First be reconciled to your brother, and then come and offer your gift' (Matt. 5:23-24). After all, we worship a pardoning God. To come before him withholding pardon demonstrates that, in one area at least, we do not aspire to be like him. The principle holds good before any encounter with God, whether hearing the Word of God, sitting at the Lord's Table or engaging in private prayer. Offences put Christians on their mettle. We are asked to pray for those who persecute us (Matt. 5:44). When someone sins against us we have an opportunity to do just that.

6. The example of Christ

There is even a challenge for believers to forgive those who do not ask for it. Jesus did so on the cross and Stephen followed his Master's example as they stoned him. This is by no means the same as acting as though no offence had been given, but it can mean that we do not react to the sins of others by sinning ourselves. How many churches have been rendered ineffective by an indignant refusal to be reconciled? How many Christians' testimony has been neutralized because a quarrel rumbles below the surface like a dormant volcano that could erupt at any moment?

With this in mind, let us see how Paul built his case that Philemon should forgive Onesimus.

Philemon owed it to Paul

1. The one who made the appeal

The phrase, **'though I might be very bold'**, is not the best translation of the first part of verse 8. It would be better rendered, 'though I have the freedom in Christ'. Paul had the right, as an apostle, to assert his authority and issue a command. Even so, it is not always a wise strategy to do so. Pulling rank may exact compliance. It does not always win hearts. With this in mind, Paul made his appeal **'for love's sake'** (9). He wore his authority lightly. We see the same logic in verse 17, where he appealed to Philemon on the basis of their partnership in the gospel to treat the runaway just as he would the respected apostle.

Note Paul's description of himself as **'Paul, the aged'** (9). It is sometimes argued that this should read, 'Paul the ambassador'. There is only the difference of one Greek letter between 'aged' and 'ambassador', but given his stated reluctance to throw his weight about, a touching appeal to his age is more likely than an assertion of his status as a herald of the gospel. By now Paul was almost sixty years old, a good age in the first century. But, as well as the tally of years, there was also the wear and tear of a life lived at full stretch for the cause of Christ. How could Philemon refuse the man who had been through all the sufferings listed in 2 Corinthians 11:22-33?

Paul also described himself as **'a prisoner of Jesus Christ'** (9). This was not an attempt to milk sympathy from Philemon. The man who saw himself as a prisoner of Christ, rather than a prisoner of Caesar, was not consumed with self-pity. It was simply a reminder that the one who made this tender appeal had earned the right to ask for high standards of discipleship from others.

2. The sacrifice Paul was making in sending Onesimus back

Furthermore, it was not easy for Paul to let Onesimus go. Life would have been much easier for a man under house arrest, as Paul was, if a willing helper could run errands, perform acts of kindness and provide companionship. It is clear from verse 13 that Onesimus had been just the help that Paul needed. Indeed, the new convert had endeared himself to Paul so much that losing him would be like tearing his heart out (12). There was clearly now a strong bond of affection between the veteran evangelist and church-planter and the young disciple. Paul's tact and sensitivity are very evident in verse 14. Paul's life would have been considerably easier if Onesimus had stayed in Rome, but Philemon had his rights, and Paul was anxious to respect them. This would not have been lost on Philemon.

3. Philemon's debt to Paul

Nor would the fact that the old apostle was willing to stand guarantor for the runaway have been lost on Philemon. There is a strong hint in verse 18 that Onesimus had financed his flight to Rome by stealing something from his master. As slaves were rarely well paid, when they were paid at all, it is likely that no amount of honest work after his conversion would have earned enough to cover the debt, so, in a post-script written in his own hand, Paul offered to cover Phi-lemon's losses himself (19). In any case, while the runaway slave might owe Philemon money, it seems that Philemon was also converted through Paul's ministry and therefore owed the apostle his place in heaven and, in a sense, his very self.

4. Paul's anticipated visit to Colosse

Finally, it is clear from verse 22 that Paul expected his appeal to Caesar to be decided in his favour, which would mean his being released from house arrest. He hoped to come to Colosse in due course and make his base in Phi-lemon's home. It would be difficult for Philemon to have the apostle in his **'guest room'** while knowing that he had disappointed the veteran saint in his request for Onesimus to be forgiven.

It would take a heart of stone to resist an appeal like this from a man like Paul, but the same apostle makes the same appeal to all believers: 'Be kind to one another, tender-hearted, forgiving one another, even as God in Christ forgave you' (Eph. 4:32).

Philemon owed it to Onesimus

If the runaway had been defiant, only going back to Colosse under duress, caution on Philemon's part might have been understandable, but one of the things that makes this short letter impressive is the testimony that it gives to the power of the gospel to change lives. Onesimus was now a very different person. Like all true Christians, he had experienced the new birth. He had been **'begotten'** while Paul was in chains (10). In the meantime he had become a consistent and gracious Christian. His helpfulness to Paul is quite apparent from the way that the apostle expressed a desire to retain his friendship and services in verse 13.

This helps to explain the pun on his name in verse 11. Onesimus means 'useful' or 'profitable'. It was typical of the kind of aspirational name that was often given to slaves. At first Mr Useful had been quite the opposite, but now he had begun to live up to his name and Paul was confident that Philemon would share his estimate of the new convert.

Paul now saw him as a **'son'** (10). Losing him would be like losing his **'own heart'**. Philemon, therefore, must cease thinking of him as a lost investment and a nuisance, but as a **'beloved brother'** in Christ (16).

Paul's appeal is essentially this: 'Philemon, Onesimus is not the man who wronged you. He is now a new man altogether. Please love him for what grace has made him.' Surely the same appeal holds good for relationships between Christians? The niggly faults of believers sometimes help us forget that every fellow Christian is a new person who is increasingly becoming Christlike. Each local fellowship is made up of new people with new natures. There is a good reason to be forbearing with what remains of the old nature in us!

Philemon owed it to himself

Paul hoped to gain much encouragement from Philemon's response. He writes of **'joy ... in the Lord'** and refreshment of **'heart in the Lord'** (20) arising out of Philemon's **'obedience'** (21). But Paul did not merely anticipate rejoicing

over the outcome, over getting what he had asked for and
gaining a happy result for Onesimus. While he would be
pleased that the prodigal's return had been met with forgiveness and acceptance as a Christian brother, he also hoped to
enjoy the growth in Philemon that made such an outcome
possible. Onesimus is not the only trophy of grace mentioned
in this passage. His is not the only example of a changed life.
We see the same power at work in Philemon, a man who was
clearly committed to striving for spiritual excellence. Paul's
appeal to him was essentially this: 'Given what you are and
the kind of Christian you want to be, rise to the challenge
and embrace the former disgrace as a brother.'

This kind of logic is very compelling. If I mean to be a
real Christian, and not just a spiritual dabbler, I will have to
swallow my pride in all sorts of ways. This might include
embracing someone who has wronged me.

Philemon owed it to God

Woven into Paul's argument is the amazing providence of
God in waylaying Onesimus, so that the man who **'departed'** from Philemon's home (15) now returned as a
Christian man and a brother (16). Onesimus made a free
choice to leave, but God overruled in grace and three lives
were changed for the better. Onesimus himself became a
child of God; Paul received a helper and companion; and
now Philemon, if he could bring himself to acknowledge it,
had another brother in Christ.

Surely Philemon would not resent such a marvellous
example of the grace of God at work and harden his heart
against the returning penitent? Would this good man begrudge a pardon for the sake of keeping his grievance warm?
In verse 8 Paul spoke of **'what is fitting'**. He had asked
Philemon to do the decent thing, the right thing. At the end

of the day, it is right that the servants of a pardoning God should forgive.

Conclusion

We don't know the outcome of Paul's appeal to Philemon, but it is hard to imagine any other ending than a handsome response on Philemon's part and a full pardon for Onesimus. Modern readers have to admit that Paul's logic has lost none of its force with the passage of twenty centuries. Nursing grudges, cherishing slights and keeping old hatreds warm is no way of life for someone who knows that his own acceptance with God was only made possible because of the blood shed for him at Calvary.

Appendix:
A word about books

The book which you have just read began its life as a series of sermon notes, when I preached through Colossians and Philemon in two stages, with a gap of roughly six months in between, in 2003 and 2004.

I found both preparing and preaching the sermons to be enormously stimulating and challenging and will be gratified if any who read this book feel that they understand the mind of Paul just a little better as a result of doing so. Those who would like to take a deeper dip would do well to consider some of the books that I used in preparation.

First of all, Geoffrey B. Wilson has written a number of books on the New Testament epistles. These were originally called 'Digests of Reformed Comment'. Each one takes the reader through the epistle in question, looking at each verse in turn. As well as commenting on the verses himself, Mr Wilson has gathered a selection of quotations from the works of great Bible scholars. Although these books are small, and therefore attractively priced, they are crammed with good things. Originally published as single volumes, Mr Wilson's commentaries have now been combined into two volumes. His treatment of Colossians is in the second volume, but the purchase of both would be money well spent. These books are produced by the Banner of Truth Trust.

One book that I found indispensable was the volume on Colossians in the excellent series published by Inter Varsity Press called 'The Bible Speaks Today'. Most series of commentaries vary in quality, but this one maintains a high standard and this particular volume by Dick Lucas is splendid. Lucas always manages to keep the main thrust of Paul's argument well to the fore.

An excellent, not to say outstanding, 'heavyweight' commentary is the one written by Peter T. O'Brien and published by Nelson in their 'Word Biblical Commentary' series.

There is also a useful volume in Eerdmans' 'New International Commentary of the New Testament' series (NICNT), written by F. F. Bruce, which also includes coverage of Paul's letter to the Ephesians.

The volume on Colossians in William Hendriksen's 'New Testament Commentary' series, published by Banner of Truth, is also worth having.

What is sometimes called 'the Colossian Heresy' is actually quite difficult to pin down, but it does seem to have had the effect of making ordinary Christians feel insecure by suggesting to them that their experience of God was second-rate compared with that of those who had undergone an experience of 'fulness'. It is not unusual to meet emphases that have the same effect in the modern scene, particularly those that come from a certain stable of teaching about the Holy Spirit and the believer's experience of sanctification. One book that is both a superb antidote to such views and a great challenge to Christian excellence in its own right is the classic *Holiness* by J. C. Ryle, which is published by Evangelical Press. This book is both a very straightforward and a very demanding read. On the one hand, it is straightforward in the sense that Ryle always writes with great clarity and in a plain, unadorned style. It is demanding, on the other hand, because it challenges the reader with a forceful presentation of what true holiness is and presses him to seek it.

Three other recent books by Evangelical Press deserve attention. *This Little Church Went to Market* by Gary Gilley is an introduction to some of the ways in which evangelical Christianity is under threat from influences from the wider world at the present time. Mr Gilley has followed this with a second book that addresses the issue of how churches are to remain faithful in a deceptive age. It is called *This Little Church Stayed Home.* The new teachers in Colosse had an unhealthy preoccupation with angels. This is also a feature of some parts of the contemporary evangelical scene. Roger Ellsworth's new book, *What the Bible teaches about Angels*, provides a healthy dose of biblical sanity on this subject.

During the course of this book I have mentioned the story of Corrie Ten Boom. The first part of her story, together with touching glimpses of her family, is told in *The Hiding Place*, published by Bantam.

Notes

Chapter 1 — Paul greets the Colossians
1. E.g. Hebrews 6:10-12; 1 Peter 1:3-8.

Chapter 2 — Paul prays for the Colossians
1. Marcus Aurelius, who reigned from AD 161–180. He featured in the block-buster movie, *Gladiator*. Christians were persecuted during his reign. One noted victim was Justin Martyr.

Chapter 3 — The incomparable Christ
1. This quotation is taken from the English Standard Version (ESV), which follows the earlier Revised Standard Version (RSV). The New King James Version (NKJV) follows the Authorized Version (AV) rendering, that it was the Father who was pleased that fulness of Godhead had taken up residence in his Son.

Chapter 4 — An incomparable salvation
1. For readers outside the United Kingdom, I am referring here to the city's soccer club, whose recent history has involved alternate promotions and relegations between the top two divisions of the English Football League system.

Chapter 9 — Don't belittle conversion!
1. Also spelled Caractacus, a British chieftain who led resistance to the Roman invasion ordered by the Emperor Claudius in AD 43. He was eventually captured and put on display in Rome.

Chapter 10 — Don't be intimidated!
1. The name used in Britain for what Americans would call a 'movie theatre'.

Chapter 11 — Don't let yourself be defrauded!
1. Croagh Patrick is a mountain in County Mayo in the West of Ireland, named in honour of St Patrick. On the last Sunday in July each year over 25,000 pilgrims make the ascent, many of them barefoot.
2. I have refrained from mentioning his name as his position seems to have changed in the years since that time.

Chapter 13 — Be heavenly-minded!
1. Richard Sibbes (1577–1635) was a minister of the gospel during the golden age of English Puritanism. He ministered at Gray's Inn in London and was Master of

St Catherine's College, Cambridge. He was the author of the spiritual classics, *The Bruised Reed and the Smoking Flax*, *The Returning Backslider* and *The Soul's Conflict*.

2. Samuel Rutherford (1600–1661) was a spiritual giant on several levels. He is best known today for his *Letters*, many of them written during a period of internal exile in Aberdeen.

3. Robert Murray M'Cheyne (1813–43) was minister of St Peter's Church in Dundee. Although he was only twenty-nine when he died, the quality of his devotional life had a lasting impact on many of his colleagues in the ministry, many of whom were among the founders of the Free Church of Scotland.

4. The coast of Cornwall, in the far south-west of the mainland of Great Britain, is particularly rugged. In the days before lighthouses were erected to warn seamen of dangerous rocks and shoals, shipwrecks were very common. The local people were very poor and regarded wrecked ships as fair game for looting. Sometimes ships were deliberately lured into danger by showing a false light.

Chapter 14 — Take no prisoners!
1. He was not, in fact, a Scot but came, as I do, from County Durham in the north-east of England.

2. This English word is taken from the Greek, *'barbaroi'*, a disparaging term intended to indicate that non-Greeks spoke unintelligible gibberish, as though they said nothing more profound than 'Bah, bah, bah…'

Chapter 15 — A new set of clothes
1. Many Christians have received a priceless education in Christian doctrine through a lifetime spent singing the best hymns.

2. In this respect the ESV follows the earlier RSV.

Chapter 16 — The Christian home
1. William Gouge, *Domestical Duties* (1634), p.331.

Chapter 17 — The Christian in the workplace
1. The trade in African slaves was given this name because the ships engaged in it made three voyages. The first was from Britain to West Africa to pick up their human cargo. The second was the 'Middle Passage' across the Atlantic to the American colonies and the third was the trip home with goods like sugar, cotton and tobacco.

2. He worked with the Soldiers and Airmen's Scripture Readers' Association (SASRA), a society with a fine pedigree of sharing the gospel with military personnel.

Chapter 19 — A capacity for friendship
1. It is the word *'diakonos'*, which lies behind the English word 'deacon'.

2. Of course, many Christians still meet in homes. In the West this is often out of preference, whereas in some parts of the world, for instance modern China, it is because the first-century realities of poverty and persecution are still all too real.

Chapter 20 — The kind of man who can forgive
1. I.e., soccer.